THE CANCER CONQUEROR

with
Bible Study Guide

For:

THE CANCER CONQUEROR

with
Bible Study Guide

GREG ANDERSON
&
MICHAEL D. GINGERICH

The Cancer Conqueror was first published in hardcover in 1988.

BTP 1098765432

Library of Congress Cataloging-in-Publication Data

Anderson, Gregory B., 1947 -
Gingerich, Michael D., 1956 –

The cancer conqueror with bible study /
Greg Anderson and Michael Gingerich

ISBN 0-9678411-3-5

1. Cancer—Psychosomatic aspects. 2. Cancer—
Psychological aspects. 3. Cancer—Spiritual
aspects. I. Title.

RC262.A66 1988   88-20502
616.99'40019—dc19   CIP

CONTENTS

AUTHOR'S PREFACE

To cancer patients . . . present and future. This book is offered to help transform your moments of fear and despair into a life of love and hope. I am now twenty years cancer-free. This, after being told by my surgeon I had just thirty days to live. I believe this is imminently possible for you.

In this book, I offer you three reflections on survival:

Survivors change. Survivors come to understand that fighting cancer is not enough. Survivors create wellness. Survivors change their diet, exercise often, choose an upward look, and create moments of pure joy and bliss, in both their work and play. Survivors change. They create wellness in body, mind and spirit.

Survivors forgive. Survivors make a sincere and disciplined effort to carry no unresolved ill-will toward anyone. Anyone. That frees body, mind and spirit for healing.

Survivors connect. Survivors come to see themselves in intimate relationships with others and especially with God.

Discover these life-transforming principles. Live in God's grace, understanding that God knows us and loves us and loves us even though he knows us.

Become these truths. When you do, you too will become a cancer conqueror.

Keep looking up,

Greg Anderson
Hershey, Pennsylvania, U.S.A.
Fall 2004

SECTION 1

The Search for Solutions

*O*nce there was a man who had just received a diagnosis of cancer.

The man did not want cancer. He wanted to be cured, to be disease-free. He wanted to live a full and happy life.

To him, cancer was a frightening enemy. And the fear it brought was a sinking feeling in his stomach that death was just about to overtake him. Was this all there was to life? There was so much left undone, so much that might have been. Maybe that was the worst part of all.

"Why me?" He had taken care of himself throughout his fifty years. Oh, he didn't always eat exactly the right foods and sometimes didn't get enough sleep. But certainly he never abused his body. Several of his friends were much worse by comparison.

And what did all this mean medically? It was bad enough to think that there might be only a short life ahead. But maybe even worse, maybe a long life of incapacitation. What would that be like?

His mind raced. "How could this happen to me? I'm losing control." It all seemed so frightening, so futile.

In the meantime, the man looked for someone who had already walked the same path, someone who had found the answer and who might be willing to share his or her experience.

First the man began asking the medical team. His family doctor had referred him to a number of medical specialists, but the one person whom the man trusted the most was his oncologist. This particular doctor was highly respected in the community as well as the medical field. He was directing the man's treatment—a plan that included a surgeon, a radiation oncologist, and other professionals.

The man inquired about his chances for successful recovery.

"Excellent," replied the oncologist. "We have every reason to believe that surgery removed the tumor and that chemotherapy will act as a doublecheck."

This was all reassuring. But he still felt a gnawing sense of fear. So many more questions remained unanswered.

He wished he could talk to someone who had been through a similar experience.

Once he found a long-term survivor, but she looked as if she might die any minute. Even though she had survived for five years—the standard "you are cured" time frame—her quality of life was less than desirable. The man wasn't looking for that.

The man knew that for his sake, as well as for the people around him, he had to find his answer soon.

Then he remembered a co-worker who, several years ago, had lived through cancer. And the interesting thing about his friend's experience was that the cancer journey seemed to have changed him—much for the better. Not only was this man's cancer under control, but he was leading a new and better life than ever before.

Maybe I should talk to him right away, thought the man. When he called his friend's home, one of the children said her parents were on a trip and wouldn't return for another three weeks. *Then he certainly must be doing well,* decided the man.

He asked the friend's daughter, "Do you know what doctor your father went to?"

"No," she replied, "I don't know the doctor. But I do know that he spent the most time with the Cancer Conqueror."

"The *Cancer* Conqueror?" asked the man.

"Yes," answered the daughter. "That's the affectionate name we gave to a man and a group of his friends who taught my dad and our family about cancer. We learned that people can conquer cancer and, in doing so, may even cure it."

The man felt a positive, supportive attitude from the girl when she asked, "Do you have cancer?"

"Yes," said the man. "How can I get in touch with the Cancer Conqueror?"

He took down a telephone number, thanked the daughter, and smiled. "How is your father now?" he asked.

"Never been better," said the daughter. "Cancer has changed our whole family's life all for the better."

"Thank you," said the man as he hung up.

This was more than a little strange. Cancer making changes for the better in the life of an entire family? That was a little hard to believe. Yet the daughter sounded so sure. Maybe there was something to be learned from this terrible thing called cancer after all.

The man called the Cancer Conqueror that same morning and they made an appointment for the following afternoon. He couldn't wait to meet the Cancer Conqueror.

SECTION 2

The Perspective of Personal Responsibility

*F*rom the moment the man arrived at the home of the Cancer Conqueror, he felt an excitement and warmth he could not explain. And the feeling was reinforced when the Cancer Conqueror answered the door with a warm greeting and an easy smile.

So this was the Cancer Conqueror! He had such an approachable manner about him. And his smile—it seemed to come as much from his eyes as from his mouth.

The two men made their way to a lovely backyard where some chilled juice had been prepared for them. They pulled up comfortable chairs, and the Cancer Conqueror asked the man to describe briefly his disease and the prognosis.

Then the Cancer Conqueror asked, "Do you have a high level of confidence in your medical team?"

"Yes," said the man, "I believe they are very knowledgeable and that they have the latest in available technology."

"Excellent. The basis for my recovery also started with a fine medical team. I had a great deal of confidence in their abilities and in them as individuals, too. But I insisted that they share all information with me in terms I could understand. And I wanted explanations for each and every test. I had to be part of every treatment decision.

"What I was really doing was taking personal responsibility for my health—personal responsibility for getting well."

"I'm not sure what you mean," said the man. "What *is* personal responsibility for getting well?"

The Cancer Conqueror leaned forward and looked deeply into the man's eyes.

"Personal responsibility for getting well—for conquering cancer—is one of the most important principles in the cancer journey. If you choose this path—the cancer-conqueror path—personal responsibility will come up again and again. It is one of those cornerstone principles that supports everything else.

"Personal responsibility for health means refusing to be a victim. It means participation in recovery by recognizing and changing self-destructive beliefs and behavior. Personal responsibility for health means believing, 'I am in charge of my cancer. My cancer is not in charge of me.'

"And personal responsibility has simple logic to it. The medical team, no matter how esteemed, function largely in the role of mechanics. They are trained in terms of *body*. They can operate and prescribe treatment, but they are not responsible for our life or our health. *We* are! Nobody can get well for us. We have to do it for ourselves.

"Selecting a medical team that we have a high level of confidence in is perhaps our first responsibility after diagnosis. But once they are in place, our attention must also focus on the role of mind and spirit in this journey."

"Mind and spirit?" asked the man. "I have a physical problem, not an emotional one."

The Cancer Conqueror nodded. His smile said he understood.

"When I encountered cancer, I instinctively knew that

I
Am
In Charge
Of My
Cancer.

My
Cancer
Is Not
In Charge
Of Me.

this was not just an experience on a physical level. I knew that my mind and spirit had a role to play.

"Personal responsibility meant that if I were to live a healthy and full life, whatever the length, that decision rested not with my doctors but with me. I also realized that once my medical team made its contribution, it was my job to discover and use *all* my healing potential. That leads beyond the body to the mind and the spirit."

"Are you saying that cancer is more than just a physical disease?"

"Yes! That's exactly what I'm saying.

"You certainly have a physical problem. It is a problem with your cells. But that's just one facet, one level of the problem. As a person, a living human being, you are much more than your body. You are also your mind and your spirit. That means you can bring these resources as well as the mechanical—the body—to the problem.

"The medical team will do all they can to help the body. If you will support them with good nutrition, exercise, and rest, the body portion of the journey will be in place."

"Okay," said the man. "I'll do those things. But I'm not sure about the mind and the spirit. Can I learn?"

The Cancer Conqueror stopped and smiled. If this person really meant that question, there was hope. With the open attitude of curiosity about the mind and spirit, much could happen. The man stood an excellent chance of being a Cancer Conqueror.

"Come, let's walk," said the Cancer Conqueror. "Let me share some of my personal story."

As they walked to the gate, the man sensed that he was about to hear something special. And he was ready to listen and learn.

"It was lung cancer," said the Cancer Conqueror. "The doctor put his hand on my shoulder and said that surgery

Cancer
Is More
Than Just
A Physical
Disease.

was the only answer. The lung would have to come out.

"They performed surgery, but four months later a growth started protruding from my neck. Again, surgery. It was malignant. It had spread throughout the neck and now they could not operate. The surgeon closed the incision, ordered radiation therapy, and told me to get my affairs in order. According to statistics, I had a thirty-day life expectancy."

The man was astonished. "My chances are much better than that. How did you do it?"

The Cancer Conqueror stopped and leaned against the fence.

"After my second surgery, I was frightened and had virtually lost all hope. I believed the doctors' prognosis. The fear of life coming to a sudden end paralyzed me.

"I was sitting on the couch looking at my daughter playing with a doll. I suddenly thought, *I will not live to see her grow up.* It was the lowest point. I don't know of any point of deeper despair. Tears filled my eyes. It was over.

"The next words that came out were full of anger and fear. 'Oh God, what can I do?'

"But somehow through the tears, through the anger and the fear, a different thought came. It was as if someone were saying, 'You may not be given long to live, but *live* as long as you are given.'

"I saw a seed of hope in that thought, a seed that I knew needed special care and attention. It was a seed that provided the framework for me to work through during the countless down times. I knew that every day I had to rededicate myself to living that one day for all it was worth. And this seed is still growing.

"Looking over at my daughter, I thought, *I may not be here to love her tomorrow. But I am here today. How can I show her my love now?*

You May
Not Be
Given Long
To Live,

But Live
As Long
As You
Are Given.

"This is the core of conquering cancer."

"That sounds so simplistic," said the man. "Isn't there more?"

"Much more," agreed the Cancer Conqueror. "This was merely the tip of an enormously powerful discovery. But living for today, doing the best I could to make love my aim, here and now, had a tremendous message of hope for me. It changed not only my health, but my entire life as well. And it can do the same for you.

"If you want to take this journey, your first assignment is to visit three different people over the next three weeks. You will learn about three Cancer Conqueror principles:

Believe

Resolve

Live

"If you complete the assignment, come back and we will talk about why it works and look at the real benefits of conquering cancer.

"Is it something that you would like to do?"

It all seemed so simple, as if there were some sort of formula to use and then everything would be okay.

The man wasn't sure he understood all the Cancer Conqueror had said, but he heard himself saying, "Okay, what do I have to lose?"

The Cancer Conqueror stopped and looked at the man with that now-familiar smile that came from his eyes. "All you have to lose," he said, "are your fears, angers, and guilt. I'll set up the first appointment for you.

"Over the weekend, give thought to your personal responsibility for getting well. YOU ARE IN CHARGE!"

SECTION 3

The Cancer Conqueror Believes

*T*he following Monday, the man found himself at a home just a few blocks from his own. He'd walked by here several times and remembered chuckling at the sign over the doorbell—LOVE SPOKEN HERE.

Now here he was, at this same house seeking answers that he wasn't even sure he knew the questions to. It seemed more than a little ironic.

An attractive woman opened the door. Her voice was pleasant. "Welcome, I'm Mary. I've looked forward to talking with you ever since the Cancer Conqueror called last week. He's quite a person, isn't he?" she asked as she led him to a table where she had hot water and herb teas waiting for them.

"Yes he is," said the man as he sat down. "Do you mind if I take notes?" he asked.

"That's great," said Mary. "When the Cancer Conqueror called, he said for us to cover the area of beliefs. So let's get started.

"The point of departure is to ask you a question. What do you think cancer means?"

"I'm not sure," said the man. "I know it is a serious illness that will probably end my life pretty quickly unless I do something about it. And the Cancer Conqueror said it was more than physical. To me cancer is the worst negative I have ever had to deal with."

Mary smiled. "Those are pretty common beliefs about cancer. Society has conditioned us to think negatively about cancer. And while some of that conditioning can be good, it has resulted in some serious untruths.

"The *three major untruths* we are conditioned to believe about cancer are:

1. Cancer means death.
2. Treatment is ineffective and has bad side effects.
3. Once you contract cancer, there is nothing you can do to help yourself.

"The truths about these statements are:

1. Cancer may or may not mean death.
2. Treatment is getting more effective and side effects less severe every day.
3. Once you contract cancer, there are *many* things you can do—especially spiritually, psychologically, and emotionally—to help yourself.

"The untruths lead to beliefs that result in despair. With despair there is no power. But the truths lead to hope. With hope there is *significant* power.

"What you choose to believe about cancer is crucial to your journey. Note how the truths match three belief areas—the disease itself, the treatment, and your role. Your beliefs about the disease, the treatment, and your role have incredible power over the outcome. You can choose those beliefs."

The man could see why the Cancer Conqueror wanted him to talk to Mary. She was forceful as she talked about beliefs. He actually held most of the negative beliefs Mary talked about.

"I want to believe the hopeful thoughts," admitted

You

Can

Choose

Your

Beliefs.

the man, "but I don't know if I can believe them immediately."

"Beliefs," said Mary, "sometimes don't change easily. Let's look at each one a little more closely. First, the disease itself.

"It really is a fact. Cancer is not synonymous with death. When I was diagnosed with breast cancer seven years ago, I thought I was going to die. Then I learned more about the disease. Cancer is actually cured in about half the cases. And over 80 percent of the patients who have the type of cancer I had survive for five years. The fact is, cancer does not mean death—it may or may not mean death."

The man was writing notes. Okay, that was certainly true. His cancer was not an automatic death sentence. That would be a positive belief he could keep. Just because he had cancer did not mean he was going to die. It was good to hear Mary say that.

Mary paused only long enough for him to have a sip of tea.

"The treatments are next. What do you believe about treatments?" she asked.

The man paused, "I guess I feel they are probably not very effective. And when it comes to side effects, I'm afraid of the possibilities."

Mary seemed to have had a very similar experience with her cancer journey. "I felt the same way when I started. My treatment was surgery followed by chemotherapy. I had heard only bad things about mastectomies. And chemotherapy—I believed it was a last-hope drug.

"But then the doctor gave me assurances. The surgery was more and more effective. And the same for chemotherapy. The truth was that the treatment plan was very hopeful."

"And the side effects?" asked the man.

"I was fortunate," said Mary. "Just as I was beginning the chemotherapy sessions, I read about the psychological component of side effects. Research had tracked a group of people who were given sterile water injections instead of chemotherapy, and a third of them lost their hair anyway."

"I don't understand," said the man.

"The only explanation the researchers could give for the hair loss was psychological in nature. They lost their hair because they *believed* the chemotherapy would do that to them."

"And there is more." Mary continued, allowing no lapse in the conversation. "In another group, 30 percent of the people got sick *on their way* to chemotherapy. They got sick, not after the drug had been administered, not during the administration, but *before*—at the very thought of chemotherapy.

"Of course that doesn't mean no one will ever have side effects again. But it does mean that there is a psychological component in the side effects and that we can work to control that component.

"In short, the belief we want to encourage is that the treatment is our friend. And as our friend, it is effective in helping overcome the physical part of the illness. It is fair to assume, then, that the side effects will, most likely, be very minimal."

"You're asking a lot," said the man. "I'm supposed to start chemotherapy, too. And I don't see those drugs as a friend at all."

Mary continued, "The Cancer Conqueror taught me that as a patient, I needed to believe in my treatment program even more than the physician who prescribed it did! That was a revelation to me. He went on to say that the treatment program was something I needed to get excited about. I would need to align myself with the treatment, believe in its effectiveness, and think of it as a welcome friend. I admit that I spent a lot of time nurturing this one belief."

More notes. The man was starting to see something. The Cancer Conqueror was right. There was more to cancer than just the physical.

"But even more important than beliefs about the disease, the treatment, and the side effects," continued Mary, "are the beliefs we have about our personal responsibility in the cancer journey. The beliefs about our role are very important."

"What do you mean?" asked the man.

"Beliefs are fascinating," said Mary. "For me they started with the thought that my role would be that of the submissive patient. At first I didn't think there was much else I could do.

"Then I was fortunate again. The same library where I found the facts on side effects had more information on other aspects of the cancer experience. Soon I was reading books on the role I could assume with my medical team, with the disease, and with my family. For the first time I was able to exercise some personal control over the illness. I was able to see my role as managing a total treatment program that included my medical team, my mind, and my spirit.

"I studied. I worked. I fanned the flames of my will to live," said Mary with enthusiasm that was contagious. "If there was a book, I read it. If there was a tape, I listened to it. If there was a video, I watched it. And I made notes and summaries of nearly everything on cancer. There is no question in my mind that my self-education was a vital part of the process of getting well.

"Yet as good as all those things were, as important as the self-education process was, I always kept coming back to mind and spirit. It became apparent to me that mind and spirit were the key parts of my treatment plan that were directly under my control. "It led me to what I consider one of the single most powerful beliefs that I had ever nurtured. I came to see that even though I *had* cancer, I *was not* cancer."

"Whatever do you mean?" asked the man.

Mary smiled as she explained. "I mean to say that by seeing myself not just as my body that was riddled with cancer, but by seeing myself also as my mind and my spirit which were very alive and ready to soar with energy, I was then able to make an important distinction. I was able to separate who I was as a person from what I had as a disease. I had control over my mind and spirit! And my mind and my spirit had cancer only if I allowed it.

"Who I was as a person was much more than what I had as a disease. That's what I mean when I say, 'Even though I have cancer, I am not cancer.' That is a powerful belief."

The man completed his notes. "Tell me more," he said.

"The Cancer Conqueror taught me some other beliefs," said Mary. "One of the most powerful was about the cancer cells themselves. Once I said to the Cancer Conqueror that it was terribly frightening to think of the cancer eating away inside my body. That's when he gently but forcefully corrected this false belief. I remember his words well: 'Cancer cells don't eat other cells. Cancer cells are weak and confused cells.'

"The Cancer Conqueror went on to explain that the cells themselves are not intelligent. They don't make up a bodily organ. Instead, they have gone mad. They are confused."

"That's true," said the man. "I always believed that the cancer was all-powerful. That's a dangerous untruth, isn't it?"

Even
Though
I <u>Have</u>
Cancer,

I <u>Am Not</u>
Cancer.

"Yes," Mary confirmed, "and another important belief puts new perspective on treatment.

"Right in our own bodies is the mortal enemy of cancer cells, our very own immune system. You see, it is not that the surgeons, the radiation, the chemotherapy, or other treatments are all-powerful. They themselves can't cure the cancer. No! The truth is that those treatments help the body's immune system heal itself—from within! The medical team is in a support role to the body's own healing power! Isn't that a revelation?"

The man sat contemplating what he had just heard. This was powerful! And he realized that the truth he was hearing could have a far-reaching impact on his own program for recovery. "Yes," he said, "I think I'm beginning to understand the huge significance of what you just said."

Mary went on, "The Cancer Conqueror taught me that cancer has a significant psychological, emotional, and spiritual component. We can understand more about this part by looking at stress and the way we handle it.

"You'll learn more about stress later. But the essentials are that mismanaged stress can lead to both a physical and psychological reaction that primes the body to respond. This priming is mind-controlled. Either responding inappropriately or suppressing a response can give the body confusing signals. The result is that our own immune systems become depressed and less effective in warding off potential cancer cells.

"These essentials are documented in a field of medicine called psychoneuroimmunology. Very basically, it recognizes that the mind and spirit do affect the body.

"Thoughts of fear, anger, and guilt can lead to sickness on more levels than just the physical. Yet thoughts of love, joy, and peace lead to health and well-being on more than just the physical level."

The man put all this in his notes. Most of what Mary said was new thinking for him.

The man hesitated a moment, "Does this mean I gave myself cancer?"

"No, no!" said Mary. "That's much too rigid a view. You didn't give yourself cancer. However, our inability to handle stress constructively, to resolve conflicts creatively, and to manage anxieties may have contributed to the beginning of illness. Of course, it wasn't a conscious decision. We never set out to give ourselves cancer. But yes, we may have contributed to the onset on a subconscious level.

"Now here is the hopeful part: If you believe that you may have contributed to your illness, then you must also believe that you have the power to contribute to your recovery.

"The psychological and spiritual components can work either for us or against us. The choice is ours."

The man nodded his thoughtful understanding. This belief was starting to make sense. And it was opening a door of hope.

"Perhaps understanding the context will help," Mary added. "Behind all these statements lies a revolutionary assumption that needs to be understood and believed at a deep level. The assumption is this—cancer is a process."

"I'm afraid you'll have to explain that a bit more," said the man.

"Conventional medical wisdom teaches us that cancer is a thing, a spatial entity or physical condition. My doctors talked about cancer as tumors. They talked about cancer as an abnormal state marked by those tumors. To them the word *cancer* was a noun—a thing."

"That is, of course, true," said the man.

"It is," Mary nodded. "But it is also a rather shallow

definition of cancer. For example, I once thought of a golf ball as simply a round, white sphere with dimples in its surface. But that was before I saw a golf ball that had been sliced in half.

"There was the outer white, dimpled shell all right. But there was also much more. Right under the surface was a deep red rubberized coating. This covered and secured the next layer, which was made up of tan-colored rubber bands. They were everywhere, tightly wound all around inside the ball. And in the very center was a hard, black rubber ball about the size of a large pea.

"Now for me to define a golf ball as round, white, and dimpled after having seen the cutaway ball would be incomplete. The same is true for cancer."

"I still don't understand what you are driving at," said the man.

"Just this. Examine your own cancer experience beyond just the surface appearances. Open your mind to the full dimensions of the idea that cancer is more than a physical condition. Cancer is not a disease of which you are a victim. It is a process which you can master.

"The medical community uses cancer as a noun. I encourage you to make cancer into a verb, an action verb! I challenge you to start to think, see, and feel yourself as 'cancering.'"

"*Cancering?*" asked the man.

"Yes," said Mary. "The verb *cancering* shifts our focus away from a disease we have and into the context of a process we are going through."

"Cancering," mused the man. "It has a strange sound to it."

"Good," said Mary. "That strange sound will help remind you that this is a process and that you have an important part in it."

"Will you trace this cancering process?" asked the man.

Cancer

Is Not

A Disease

Of Which

You

Are

A Victim.

It Is

A Process

Which

You Can

Master.

"Okay," said Mary, "let's walk through the typical steps.

"First, we need to understand that not every cancer patient's experience would fit this pattern. Certainly there are genetic causes of cancer. Some people are born with that unfortunate physical predisposition. And there is no question that carcinogens in our environment, in our foods, all around us, can trigger malignancy.

"Even so, there is increasing evidence that many cancers are stress-related. In fact, the percentage may be much higher than first imagined. One group of researchers in a recent study found that more than 90 percent of the participants could trace the onset of cancer to a period of high stress. The researchers went so far as to say that, in their opinion, this same percentage probably applied to nearly all cancers."

"Astounding," said the man.

"The evidence is becoming overwhelming. Many times the body will start cancering because of the prolonged emotional conflict that has its base in stress. And this emotional conflict—the feelings of loss, hopelessness, and despair—can lead to mental depression. Today scientists feel that there must be some sort of direct link between mental depression and immune system depression. The result can be the onset of disease.

"Now we need to make a careful distinction. This is not to say that all people who are having emotional distress will start cancering. No, it is to say that the cancering process often begins on the emotional level.

"Perhaps the first symptoms are barely detectable. And it may be months, even years, before physical symptoms occur. The physical symptoms eventually compel the patient to seek a medical diagnosis and a treatment plan is then developed and begun.

"And while a proper treatment program on the physical

level is mandatory, I encourage you to understand that the cancering process is far more inclusive. The physical portion—the tumor—is only a signal in the process."

The man sat silently for a moment. "My intuition accepts this. But my rational mind wants to resist it."

Mary said, "Are you assuming that cancering excludes the traditional, rational, medical approach? Cancering includes it. We are simply opening our minds to go beyond the limits of that thinking. Because the truth is, cancering is both rational and intuitive.

"Believe it, cancer doesn't just happen to us. It can spring from inner disharmony, either physical or emotional. And this has two implications. One is responsibility. We may have been responsible, at least subconsciously, for contributing to the onset of the illness.

"But the second implication is opportunity. Cancer is a reversible disease, and there are patients who happily experience reversal every day.

"Our task is to choose harmony at the level of the mind and the spirit. Only then can we help our bodies regenerate and achieve physical harmony.

"This is truly conquering cancer. And in conquering, we might even cure it."

Mary continued, "The Cancer Conqueror likes to help us reframe the meaning of cancer. By reframing, he means looking at the illness in a different light.

"And while this perspective includes new ways to consider several beliefs about the illness, the treatment, and our roles, the Cancer Conqueror encourages the primary belief that *cancer is a message to change.*

"Yes, cancer does have a physical component. And yes, it can be life-threatening. But even though this is true, cancer is foremost a warning for us to change.

"The Cancer Conqueror calls this change *resolve.* When we resolve those areas in our lives where there is unrest,

Cancer

Is A

Message

To Change.

where there is anxiety, we make changes that will nourish love, joy, and peace. That's really conquering cancer.

"And in conquering, we may even cure cancer. The body can often respond physically to renewed feelings of hope. The mind's resolution of conflicts is often followed by the body's resolution of disease. This is true because body, mind, and spirit work together as one system.

"Our task, then, becomes one of identifying those areas that need resolution, fulfilling those needs, and choosing positive options for the future.

"Cancer becomes a message to change."

The man looked at all his notes. He wanted to spend time studying the implications of all this for himself.

"I know you need time to study," responded Mary. "Work this week on replacing negative beliefs with positive beliefs. I will arrange a meeting next week for you with one of the most beautiful people you will ever meet. Her name is Barbara, and she will teach you about resolving—one of the most important steps in life reeducation and in conquering cancer."

Mary made the call; the time was set.

"Let me leave you with The Cancer Conqueror's favorite story about beliefs. One of his heroes is Christopher Columbus. At that point in history, everyone believed the world was flat. But Columbus decided to challenge that belief. He took a chance, and the world has never been the same since! He was a real conqueror!

"Our beliefs about cancer are like that. You are a modern-day Columbus about to start a journey. Some people will tell you there is no hope, that the world is flat. Don't believe it! Instead, take a chance. Start the journey. Become a cancer conqueror!

"In a real sense, what you believe about this journey is what you'll experience. You can choose—you *must* choose—your beliefs. Make certain they are beliefs that serve you well. Will those beliefs instill despair or will they inspire hope? You choose."

The man left, touched by Mary's power and authority. He was so impressed that he stopped his car down the block, got out his notebook, and made a summary of the positive beliefs right there.

POSITIVE BELIEFS SUMMARY

THE ILLNESS
1. I do not believe cancer is synonymous with death.
2. I believe cancer cells are weak and confused; they don't eat other cells.

THE TREATMENT
3. I believe treatment is very effective against these weak and confused cells.
4. I believe the side effects, if any, can be controlled.
5. I believe my own immune system overcomes cancer cells daily.

MY ROLE
6. I believe I am personally responsible for my cancer journey.
7. I believe I manage my total treatment program.
8. I believe I am "cancering." It is a process I can master.
9. I believe I can control the emotional, psychological, and spiritual aspects of the illness.
10. I believe cancer is a message for me to change.

The Cancer Conqueror Resolves

*E*arly the following week, the man was at the door of Barbara's home. The first thing he noticed about Barbara was her smile. It was that same kind of joyful expression he had seen in Mary and in the Cancer Conqueror. And Barbara's voice—it was calm and soothing, another indication of her obvious warmth. They made their way to the patio.

"How is your journey progressing?" began Barbara.

"Well, I've just started," replied the man. "But already the difference in my beliefs is significant. I'm less frightened of the disease. And I also feel more confident in my treatment and in my medical team."

"Excellent," said Barbara. "And where are you in terms of your role?"

"My role is the area that confuses me most. Frankly, I really doubt that what I think or feel will have much effect on the cancer. So I'm not sure about my role."

"Let's discuss that," said Barbara. "The Cancer Conqueror teaches us that much of our role is in the area he calls 'resolve.'

"Resolve starts with some real basics—diet and exercise. Good nutrition is essential for wellness. Information on sensible eating habits is available from a variety of sources. Seek this information out. Contact the National Cancer Institute for their guidelines. Consider nutritional

49

supplements. Become your own nutrition expert. Act on
the belief that what you put in your body is important.
You deserve the best in nutrition.

"And exercise. Many people have significant issues
to resolve here. Even patients with limiting conditions
can maintain an exercise program to some degree. The
benefits are both physical and psychological. The type of
exercise and the frequency are up to you. The Cancer
Conqueror personally uses a half hour three times a week
as his yardstick. I have done the same and have chosen
walking. Like your research in the area of nutrition,
study the literature and become your own exercise expert. Remember, the goal here is to feel more energized,
not to become a super athlete.

"But as important as diet and exercise are, when the
Cancer Conqueror talks about resolve, he is really putting
his emphasis on issues of a psychological and emotional
nature. In fact, he is really starting at the point of loving
ourselves. Unless we have a healthy respect for ourselves,
we probably won't eat right or exercise.

"Resolve goes much deeper than the externals of diet
and exercise. When we examine the issue of resolve, we
are really focusing on identifying and clearing our lives
of emotional roadblocks and self-destructive behavior.
This is very important because the resolve principle is
based on the premise that emotions affect us physically."

"Is that really provable?" asked the man.

"I'm not certain what you require in terms of proof,"
continued Barbara. "The whole area of psychoneuroimmunology, or PNI for short, is documenting this mind
over illness phenomenon. And it is for real. I encourage
you to be open to the possibilities in it.

"Simply stated, the Cancer Conqueror encourages us to
acknowledge that attitudes, beliefs, and thoughts go together to create a mental and emotional outlook toward

Beliefs,

Attitudes,

And

Feelings

Lead To

Illness

Or

Wellness.

life, an emotional lifestyle. Those emotions, either positive or negative, translate to the physical. Our beliefs, attitudes, and feelings lead to illness or wellness.

"Perhaps even more astounding, the Cancer Conqueror
teaches us that emotions can play a central role in cancer's
onset and course."

"Wait," interrupted the man. "You're saying things that
aren't really proven. I'm a businessman. I need proof.
Anyway, I thought we were going to talk about resolve,
not emotions."

Barbara observed his surprising resistance. How could
she break through? Could his reaction be a clue to his
problem?

While it wasn't Barbara's style to be confrontive, she
heard herself firmly telling the man, "Listen, please listen
with your mind; don't just hear with your ears."

The man stared at her. It wasn't hard to sense his
discomfort. Or was it thinly disguised anger?

"We *are* talking about resolve," continued Barbara. "But
emotions are the issue at the very core of resolve.

"I am not a medical doctor or researcher. However,
PNI experts have given us much evidence that emotions
occupy a central role in health. Consider this:

Cancer cells are regularly present in virtually all
people. Yet relatively few of these people become ill.
That is because the body's immune system is so powerful. It is the natural enemy of abnormal cells. The
immune system routinely contains or destroys these
cells, allowing them to be carried away through natural bodily processes.

"Yet, when a malignant cell is not destroyed, what is
the reason behind the immune system's not working?

What lapse in the body's defenses might allow these cells to develop into a life-threatening tumor? Why has it developed now? What may have caused the immune system to function at less than full capacity when for years it did operate so very effectively?

"Some people answer this by insisting it is a matter of genetics. Others say diet. Still others teach that it is carcinogens in the environment.

"All these may have a contribution to make in answering the question, 'Why cancer now?' But none offers a full explanation."

Barbara leaned forward and touched the man's arm. "Listen very carefully," she said. "This is perhaps as close as I will get to offering you the proof you seem to need."

The man sat quietly. Barbara continued:

"Genetics, carcinogens, and diet do play a role in the development of cancer. But why aren't they consistently the trigger? If there is genetic predisposition to cancer, it has always been there. Diet may play a part, but in all likelihood, the patient's diet has actually been rather predictable for years. And what about carcinogens? Most people have certainly been exposed to harmful substances before. So why now? What is different at this point in time that would allow the cancer to develop?

"It is at this point that PNI brings us back to the emotional components. What is different? Early research has demonstrated that the development of cancer requires more than just the presence of abnormal cells; it requires also a suppression of the body's natural defenses, the immune system.

"And the difference that could suppress the immune system? Changed emotional states."

The man was listening intently.

"Not only *changed* emotional states, but *charged* emotional states. Fear. Anger. Guilt. All negative emotional states. All commonly the result of mismanaged stress. All potentially capable of depressing the person and the immune system."

The man was starting to write some notes now. Barbara glanced down to see him circle the word *stress*.

"Much of the emotional side of cancer," continued Barbara, "can be understood in the framework of stress. Actually, the issue isn't the stress, but how we manage that stress."

"Tell me more," said the man.

"There are times that each of us faces highly stressful situations, when major emotional upsets seem to dominate our lives. For years the medical community has documented that illness is more likely to occur following highly stressful events in people's lives.

"Some illnesses and their link to stress are readily accepted by the medical community—ulcers, high blood pressure, headaches, even some heart disease. More recently, though, backaches, infections, and even accidents have been seen to increase when the person is dealing with emotional upset. Do you believe all this is true?"

"Yes," agreed the man.

"Good," said Barbara. "It *is* true. And research is finding more and more diseases that are linked to stress all the time.

"Stress can translate to changes in emotional states. Stress can challenge the way we relate to life. Perhaps it challenges our habits, relationships, or our self-image. We 'feel' these challenges—emotionally."

"Is this like the 'fight or flight' response?" asked the man.

"That's exactly it. The human body is endowed with some fantastic capabilities that protect us. When our early ancestors encountered a tiger in their path, there was an immediate reaction. Their breathing speeded up, their adrenaline flowed, and their heart beat faster. When presented with a stressful situation, the body prepared the person either to stay and battle the tiger or to get away from the area as quickly as possible. Thus, the fight or flight response.

"Now most twentieth century people don't normally have to deal with a wild animal in their path. But we do have to deal with mental tigers—all the time. And those are the stresses that can trigger the same bodily reactions.

"Instead of fighting or fleeing, which actually puts to, use adrenaline, rapid heartbeat, and faster breathing, modern-day people often suppress or even deny their response. The body's response to an emotional reaction does not get discharged. When we have no outward action available, the stress is internalized. And internalized stress can set us up for trouble.

"It's amazing. Research has found that stress is related to both negative and positive change. While an event like the death of a spouse ranks at the very top of the chart and is certainly negative, a normally positive event such as marriage also produces significant stress. The point is that both negative and positive events of life require new coping skills. Both can often be experienced as emotional conflict.

"It is not enough merely to analyze the stressful events or acquire the new coping skills. We must move to the emotions behind the stress that invariably have their roots in some form of fear, anger, or guilt."

The man was taking many notes by now.

"Then the key point becomes how we manage the emotions associated with stress. Two things must happen in successful stress management. The Cancer Conqueror calls this management the StresSolverSystem:

CHANGE YOUR PERCEPTION OF YOURSELF
AND
CHANGE YOUR PERCEPTION OF YOUR PROBLEM!

"It is really that basic. We need to change our perception of ourselves and our ability to handle whatever life problems face us, particularly the problems prior to cancer. Plus, we need to be able to perceive actual personal problems as being less threatening. Arguably, you could solve the emotional conflict with just one change in perception. But the StresSolverSystem of increasing personal power and decreasing problem power is the essence of successful stress management."

More notes. Was she breaking through?

"The outcome of mismanaged stress is, predictably, emotional conflict. And the outcome of continuing emotional conflict—chronic fear, anger, and guilt—can lead to feelings of helplessness, hopelessness, and despair. From here, it is a short step to depression."

"Okay," said the man. "But this doesn't necessarily mean I'll get cancer."

"That's correct," said Barbara. "There is no 100 percent fixed link. But PNI studies are demonstrating there is some correlation between a depressed mind and a depressed immune system."

"How is that?" pursued the man.

"The heart of the immune system is the person's white blood cells. In an amazing discovery recently, white blood cells were shown to have neuroreceptors. This means that feelings, our emotions, may be biochemically transmitted to and 'felt' by the immune system. This is significant.

StresSolverSystem

Change Your
Perception
Of Yourself
And

Change Your
Perception
Of Your
Problem.

"Just as negative and positive emotions can and do affect the human spirit, they also would seem to affect the immune system. And a chronically depressed immune system can lead to illnesses of many kinds, including cancer.

"Mind affecting body and emotions directing, or maybe even controlling, health make perfect sense. When you have previously been ill, didn't that make you feel psychologically down? In that case, body affected mind. It follows that the reverse could also be true, that mind can affect body. PNI is proving that even as we speak. This is much more than theory."

The man looked thoughtful, pondering what Barbara was saying. "It fits my case," he said. "I lost my job about a year ago. I've tried everything I can think of, but there is nothing I can do to get suitable work. It makes me so mad. I just hate my old boss. And I feel so worthless. I'm really depressed."

Barbara realized now what the problem was. What the man said gave her some of the insight she needed to assist him in resolving his particular situation. Realizing that this was a delicate task of self-discovery, she proceeded gently but firmly.

"I think I can understand how you feel. It has to be tough. But let's stop for a moment and apply what I've just said. Like it or not, losing a job doesn't make you angry. . . . You make you angry. Being fired doesn't make you feel worthless. . . . You make you feel worthless. You choose those feelings.

"Feelings of helplessness and hopelessness," said Barbara, "were at the heart of the development of my cancer. Let me share my experience. In many ways it parallels yours.

"After thirty-two years of marriage and four wonderful children, my husband and I were divorced. With no small amount of self-pity, I described it by saying, 'He just left me.' I felt fearful, angry, and worthless. Then I became depressed. I viewed myself as a victim."

"A victim under your husband's control, or just a victim out of control?" asked the man.

"Actually both," said Barbara. "And I even took it a step further. I saw myself as a victim of life. What I mean is that I let the crisis situation of the divorce touch all areas of my life. I suppose my reasoning was something like, *If I am a failure as a wife and mother, I must be a failure at everything else.* Mentally and emotionally, I took everything to its worst possible conclusion.

"I then reasoned, *If I am a failure, personally helpless in all life's areas, my life is hopeless. I am a victim of whatever life decides to serve me; a victim with a capital V.*

"I failed to realize hope and hopelessness are both a choice. And I have a personal responsibility for those choices! Why not choose hope?

"The Cancer Conqueror is currently trying to help a friend who was recently diagnosed with prostate cancer. This man adopted a victim stance that included a belief that cancer was a virtual death sentence and that he would probably become impotent as a result of treatments. This man sees himself as being trapped by events beyond his control. He views himself as having no meaningful way to deal with these issues. He is filled with despair. He has chosen an emotional outlook that recognizes only helplessness. He's become a victim to what life has given him. He has surrendered his power and personal responsibility to choose hope. This is the classic victim stance."

"That's a very descriptive illustration," replied the man. "This victim stance seems to relate to my own situation of being out of work and developing cancer, doesn't it?"

"It might," said Barbara. "You be the judge of that." She

Hope
And
Hopelessness
Are Both
A Choice.

Why
Not Choose
Hope?

was encouraged. The man was at least acknowledging the possible link between his emotional state and cancer. Barbara would carefully help him take the next step.

"For me," continued Barbara, "the victim stance actually started with my self-image, including what I was supposed to do in life. It is a typical pattern the Cancer Conqueror describes like this:

1. *A series of high-stress events tears at the person's self-image.* I am faced with divorce. My self-talk based on my self-image says, "I am 'supposed' to be married. Early in my life, I was taught that marriage and motherhood meant success. Now that I am divorced, I must be a failure."

2. *The person's self-allowed techniques for coping are inadequate in response to the self-image threat.* My self-talk says, "Life for me was 'supposed' to be as a wife and mother. I have no idea how a divorced person is 'supposed' to function. I am not in control."

3. *The person sees no way to resolve his or her emotional needs and becomes a victim.* Self-talk speaks out again, "I can't go on. The situation is hopeless. *I* am helpless."

Barbara continued, "While my divorce is a rather obvious example, all of us adopt victim stances. A person in a dead-end job is afraid to move. An abused wife is fearful of leaving an abusive mate. Even attitudes like 'That's just the way I am,' use the victim stance as a convenient way to avoid personal change and growth. In fact, we can choose to be victors instead of victims!"

"This really does relate to my being out of work," said the man. "I once viewed myself as being productive and successful. That became my self-image. That was *me!* When I was dismissed—I just hate to use the word 'fired'—my whole reason for living ceased to exist. And I was defenseless. There was nothing I could do. I felt powerless. Life became unmanageable. And anger ruled

We Can
Choose
To Be
Victors

Instead Of
Victims!

to the point of rage. I was, and I guess I feel I still am, that victim. I sometimes feel so out of control."

Wow, Barbara thought to herself, *this could be a turning point! He has opened his mind to renewal.* The man's words had come fast and with such emotional force. This was excellent!

She spoke ever-so-sensitively, "You have just taken what is perhaps the most difficult step in conquering cancer. None of us wants to concede weakness or helplessness. But by doing so, you have opened yourself to wonderful possibilities. You can transform this attitude into self-renewal."

The two sat silently for several moments.

"But what do I do?" continued the man. "I still feel so vulnerable. It's terrifying!"

Vulnerable didn't come close to describing how he really felt. He was emotionally naked. He had bared his soul to a virtual stranger. He didn't even talk to his wife about some of these feelings. It was frightening to be so open. He realized Barbara was answering his question, and he struggled to focus his mind on what she was saying.

"What you do now is begin to work on renewing your mind and your emotions. The victim stance is full of fears, angers, and guilts. *They* are what you'll work on first. That is what conquering cancer is all about, taking personal responsibility for changing our negative emotions."

The man was reflective as he tried hard to understand some of the implications of what Barbara was telling him.

"I'm not good at expressing my emotions," admitted the man. "I have always believed that some feelings were best left unsaid. In fact, my father always said that people who talk about them seem pretty weak."

"Interesting that you should say that," said Barbara. "The Cancer Conqueror helped me so much when he shared the three most consistent traits of the cancer-prone personality:

"First, the typical cancer personality has a tendency to **bottle up emotions**. You've just shared your thoughts on how you express your feelings as 'best left unsaid.' In my case," continued Barbara, "I tended to play 'poor me' and go into a prolonged silence."

The man chuckled. "I've done some of that."

"We all have," said Barbara. "And it is related to the second tendency, excessive **difficulty grieving loss**. In my divorce, I felt as if I had been done the ultimate wrong. I felt abandoned by my husband. And when the children wouldn't take my side, I felt totally unappreciated. It was an overwhelming sense of loss. And I continued living with those feelings until the Cancer Conqueror began to work with me on expressing my grief over those losses."

The man responded, "I've never thought of my job loss in terms of grief. I suppose that is one framework in which to analyze it, though. I do know it has been a very difficult year. And I feel profoundly empty. I suppose some mourning is taking place inside."

Barbara nodded her agreement; she was encouraged. The man was trying. He was working at this very sensitive assignment. And he was making progress. She continued:

"The third most common characteristic of a typical cancer profile is **judgmentalism**, being unduly critical of others. No question—I certainly did that, particularly where it concerned my husband. In fact, I'm ashamed to say that I really went through life being critical of others. It was a twisted attempt to pull myself up by pushing others down."

The man was contemplative. "I suppose I carry some of all three personality traits."

"Perhaps," said Barbara. "Those personality character-
istics can lead to fear, anger, and guilt that can depress
the immune system and allow cancer, and other illnesses,
to flourish."

"Here we are again. I keep thinking I caused my own
cancer!" sighed the man.

"Recall our beliefs?" asked Barbara. "Just remember
that we probably did contribute to the illness on a subconscious level.

"But the real key is this: If you acknowledge that you
may have contributed to the illness, then, by definition,
you must also acknowledge that you have the ability to
contribute to your wellness."

"I do remember," said the man. "I need to find out how
I contributed negatively. Then it follows that I can reverse it and contribute to health positively."

"Exactly! Excellent!" said Barbara. "Remember, cancer
is a reversible disease. You can contribute to that reversal."

"That's powerful!" said the man.

The man thought, *This is simple yet so profound. On an
intuitive level, the mind-affects-body principles make sense.
And if science can't accurately explain electricity, yet em-
braces it, why do I demand a full explanation of psychoneuroimmunology? I want to reverse my disease. I want LIFE!*

"Okay," said the man. "I want to get well! I'm choosing
life! Where do I start to resolve?"

Barbara beamed! *Choosing life!* Those words affirming
the will to live were powerful. Perhaps he had turned the
corner in his thinking.

"You've already started," smiled Barbara. "What you
do next is take a rigorous emotional inventory of yourself.
The Cancer Conqueror gives us three questions that, if
treated with seriousness, will lead us to higher self-
awareness. You'll want to take notes here.

Cancer

Is A

Reversible

Disease.

"First, ask yourself **what high-stress, emotionally disruptive events happened to you in the year or two prior to diagnosis?** This is the stress-management issue. High-stress events can be identified in many patients. But what the Cancer Conqueror really wants us to do is get in touch with the way we reacted to those events. Did we respond to the events with paralyzing fear? Or did we get angry and let anger turn to smoldering resentment? Or did guilt cause such a sense of shame that we may have felt we deserved some kind of punishment? And given the perspective of time, can we now look at different and more constructive ways of handling the situation?

"Second, **what emotional needs might you be meeting or masking with the cancer?**"

"What do you mean?" asked the man.

"Just this. Cancer gets you cards and get well wishes from friends and relatives. It can certainly get you out of work. You can stay at home in bed. It gets you attention, no small amount of sympathy, and may even serve as a means of obtaining nurturing from an otherwise non-nurturing spouse. Just think of that power!

"Cancer is a great permission-giver, allowing both patient and family an acceptable reason to say no to the demands of others. It can also provide a reason to say yes to things that have been put off or otherwise neglected in a person's life."

"I've never really thought about cancer that way before," said the man.

"The Cancer Conqueror," continued Barbara, "calls these cancer games. His real point is to get us to look at the motivation behind our illness-related behavior. It is a fact—in our society sickness is a very powerful force, one that is often rewarded. Patients can manipulate that force, misusing it to meet their needs. Some people emotionally cling to the disease. It's their newfound way of fulfilling emotional needs that otherwise have gone unmet."

"That seems incredible to me," said the man.

"Incredible but true," said Barbara. "You will be invited to join a group of us who meet regularly. There you will meet a woman who not only has cancer, but in her lifetime has had nine elective surgeries, currently takes eleven different prescriptive medications, and claims this is the best she has felt in twenty-five years!

"She may be feeling better now than at anytime in the last twenty-five years, but the fact that she still recounts her many illnesses over and over again is a give-away that she probably is manipulating her disease. It's her best way of getting love and even some attention from her otherwise angry and resentful husband.

"The Cancer Conqueror brings us back again and again to this point of examining what needs we might be meeting or masking with the illness. 'Why do I need this illness?' and 'What am I gaining from this illness?' become important issues for us to understand fully. I encourage you to spend all the time you need here.

"This leads to the third question, **what healthy options might you choose to fulfill these needs?** Emotional needs are real. Denying them has probably been part of our problem. The Cancer Conqueror encourages us to recognize the real needs that we feel; he encourages us to look at them squarely and not deny them. He also gives us permission to fulfill those needs but encourages us to do it in a positive, healthy way."

"In the next step of your journey, you'll study LIVE. The whole thrust there is to suggest positive ways, indeed a whole healthy lifestyle, that will meet these needs and contribute to your total wellness.

"But first, let's complete this issue of resolve. Here is an important point. I give you permission to give yourself permission to make certain your needs are met! What do you suppose is your number one need?"

"Mine is simple. I need a job," said the man.

"Wait," said Barbara persuasively. "Look more deeply than that. What are you really after?"

"What do you mean?" he asked.

"Let me offer some examples. In my case," continued Barbara, "I felt I needed to be married. Then the Cancer Conqueror helped me see that what I was really after was feeling loved. But I was going about achieving that goal in a strange and self-destructive way. I was measuring the fulfillment of my love needs by the amount of attention and affection I received.

"When I did that, I always set myself up for disappointment; my husband and children could satisfy those needs only for short periods of time. And when I didn't receive attention and affection, I doubted my self-worth and began to fear being rejected and abandoned. In my search for emotional fulfillment, I manipulated the people most dear to me and caused them to resent me. In some ways, I can understand why my husband left even after all those years we had together.

"The Cancer Conqueror helped me resolve nearly all those issues when he said that my job was to forgive— myself and others. Then he traced how certain processes help people release resentments and forgive both real and perceived wrongs, thus opening the mind and the body to healing. In fact, the Cancer Conqueror believes this is an essential part in getting well.

"Forgiveness was a breakthrough issue for me. It was the process of letting go of the thoughts I had harbored about people who I perceived were harming me. It was equally a process of letting go of the thoughts I had kept about my harming others.

"I no longer saw myself as always being right and

My Job
Is To
Forgive —
Myself
And
Others.

others as always being wrong. I was not innocent and others guilty. That thinking had put me into the blame game where I was seeing myself as a victim, not responsible for my own emotional choices. I was surrendering that power over myself to others. What a mistake! Now I could choose differently. Now I could look upon myself and others with love.

"In fact, for the first time I realized others were doing the best they could, given their level of awareness. And that applied to me as well. The issue was not blame at all.

"I remember one exercise that was most helpful. The Cancer Conqueror had us write out a blame list. We wrote out individuals names, and next to it what we blamed them for. Interestingly, the first name on the list had to be our own. Then, in a joyful ceremony, we all crumpled our lists up in a ball and threw them in a trash can. Then we took the trash cans outside and burned the lists. It was marvelous! It is an event that is vividly etched in my memory, and to this day, it helps me to stop blaming and start forgiving.

"Forgiveness became an important vehicle—a major tool for me to use in the resolve process. I actively forgave others. In fact, I wished them well and imagined good things happening to them. It was really wonderful. And I forgave myself. I realized I could feel loved whether I was married or single, whether my children sided with me or my husband. I realized that my feeling loved was not dependent on others showing me attention or affection. It was instead dependent upon my showing love to others. Whenever I did, I felt loved. And I believe that by resolving this emotional conflict, I helped my body heal itself. Does that make sense? Does that fit you?" asked Barbara.

"I'm not sure," pondered the man quietly.

"For me," Barbara went on, "the real need was to

replace fear, anger, and guilt with love, joy, and peace. 'Being married' and 'needing to feel loved' were only symptoms of a deeper need. Perhaps that is what you're really after.

"Time after time the people who conquer cancer are the ones who work systematically at resolving their emotional conflicts. The main issues are accepting personal responsibility on all levels of life, frank examination of fundamental beliefs, better management of stress, improving self-image, and nurturing better relationships through loving and forgiving. There's more, but that's the heart of it.

"I believe a cancer conqueror needs to get to the point where he or she says, 'I value myself and I am unwilling to remain miserable. I will no longer live life this old destructive way. I will change.'"

The man was thoughtful as he finished his notes, ". . . unwilling to remain miserable; . . . a new person."

"Your experience of extended unemployment is common. I'm thinking of a man who is part of our Cancer Conqueror group who was also fired from his job. He was a senior officer in one of the largest companies in this city. In fact, his departure was carried in the newspapers. He felt disgraced. His entire self-image was centered around his job. And within one year, cancer.

"He spent time with the Cancer Conqueror, who helped him analyze his resentment. 'I'm so mad because I don't have a job,' he said. The Cancer Conqueror helped him realize a new truth—perhaps he didn't have a job because he was so mad. He had to grasp his real need. For years he had harbored resentment. It was time to change—not just jobs, but some deep emotions."

The man listened intently as Barbara continued.

Our
Emotions
Don't
So Much
Happen
To Us;

We
Choose
Them.

"It's tough to deal with those emotions. They are at the heart of where we live every day. Just remember that our emotions don't so much happen to us; we choose them."

"That's an odd thought," said the man.

"At first it may seem odd, but examine it. When my husband and I went through our divorce, I was the classic victim. Then cancer. The illness merely reinforced my victim stance. I became a servant of my fears, angers, and guilts. I *chose* negative emotions.

"It wasn't until the Cancer Conqueror helped me reframe these negative emotions and taught me forgiveness that I was able to realize I could actually determine my own emotions. I realized I wasn't a captive of my fear, anger, and guilt—instead I was, or at least could choose to be, a product of love, joy, and peace.

"For the first time, I realized that we can't control life but we can control our *response* to life. And I also saw cancer as a message—as negative feedback—that up to now, I had not been making all the right choices. I changed. I chose life. I chose to LIVE!"

The man remained silent, deep in thought.

Barbara paused for a moment and when the man was ready, she continued, "It all brings us back to the core of resolve—the changing of our emotional lifestyles. By doing that, we prepare the body to heal. Clearing our lives of emotional difficulty is a LIVE message. This is resolving!"

"It's interesting," said the man. "Resolve isn't changing the circumstances so much as changing ourselves."

"Precisely," said Barbara. "We can't ever change anyone but ourselves. That is the key. It's true. I became a cancer conqueror not because I went into remission—instead, I became a cancer conqueror because I chose to become a new person!"

Another pause. More reflection.

You Become A
Cancer Conqueror
Not Because
You Go Into
Remission —

Instead,
You Become A
Cancer Conqueror
Because You Choose
To Become
A New Person!

"It all sounds so easy," said the man.

Barbara smiled, "Nobody will tell you it is easy. Simple? Yes. Easy? No. Just try to remember that change, like our emotions, is a choice. New choices are not easy. Pain is inevitable, but suffering is optional."

"Oh, that's good," said the man. "That's an excellent perspective. But how do I actually *do* all this? How do I make these changes real for me?"

Barbara reached for a piece of paper and began writing. "Here is the name and telephone number of a fellow journeyer. John has a whole new and exciting message for you to consider. And it is all centered on how to make these concepts work in your life. Call him and set up an appointment after you have begun to work through some of the resolve principles."

"I will," promised the man. "But before we quit today, will you help me summarize the principles we covered under resolve?"

"Of course," said Barbara. "Let's make a list."

RESOLVE SUMMARY

1. Emotions affect us physically.
2. Beliefs, attitudes, and feelings lead to illness or wellness.
3. Fear, anger, and guilt can depress the immune system.
4. The StresSolverSystem: I increase my personal power and decrease my problem power.
5. Hope and hopelessness are both a choice. Why not choose hope?
6. Instead of choosing to be a victim, I can choose to be a victor.

7. Cancer is a reversible disease.
8. My job is to forgive—myself and others.
9. Our emotions don't so much happen to us; we choose them.
10. You become a cancer conqueror not because you go into remission—instead, you become a cancer conqueror because you choose to become a new person!

SECTION 5

The Cancer Conqueror LIVES

*T*he man spent an uncomfortable week trying to deal with the issues of resolve. It proved to be no easy task. And the man also had to admit he did not fully appreciate having to work on emotional conflicts. *It gets you in touch with some heavy issues. Aren't these things best left buried?* he thought. This was tough and frightening as well.

The man made a lunch appointment with John to talk about LIVE. Perhaps this would be an easier assignment. Maybe John would be able to help him through the difficult process of changing.

The man arrived at John's offices early. The receptionist pointed to an open double door and said, "You'll find him right in there. Go in."

As the man entered, he saw John not behind his desk but standing in front of it juggling three balls. "Come in," smiled John as soon as he saw the man. "Let's see how long I can keep these up!"

John's personality immediately drew a stranger in. Along with it came a big, easy smile and a nonpresumptive manner. Yet John's clothes, his grooming, and his posture also commanded a certain respect for this unusual businessman. Here was someone you liked and wanted to know more about.

"Oops!" laughed John as one of the balls dropped to

the floor. "I'm going to practice more tomorrow! Hello! Welcome!" he smiled as they shook hands.

John's deep voice was melodious. "I've had some fruit brought in for us," he said as he gestured to the conference table. "Let's just eat right here. Make yourself at home."

After only a couple of minutes of pleasantries, John said, "You impress me as a person of much intelligence. And because of that, I am going to take a chance. I'm first going to tell you a story that I believe will help you always to recall the central point of LIVE."

"Okay," chuckled the man, "go ahead." You just had to like John. His directness was refreshing and nonoffensive. Besides, how could you fault somebody who had already noticed your intelligence—someone who must be a keen observer of human talent? No doubt about it, John was joyful. He smiled as he began his story.

"Once upon a time there was a handsome prince.

"One day this handsome prince was on a walk in the forest when he met a wicked witch.

"The mean, old, wicked witch was very evil. She waved her magic wand and turned the handsome prince into a frog.

"As the wicked witch was leaving the forest, she said, 'The only way this spell can be broken is with a kiss from a beautiful fair maiden.'"

John continued, the big smile widening across his face. He was having fun!

"One day a beautiful fair maiden came to the edge of the stream where the prince-disguised-as-frog lived. Seeing his chance, he spoke to the beautiful fair maiden, telling her of his plight. 'And as the wicked witch left,' he finished, 'she told me that the only way the spell could be broken would be by a kiss from a beautiful fair maiden. Will you kiss me and turn me back into a prince?'

"The princess looked at him. Certainly she didn't *feel* like kissing a frog. How could she really know if he were telling the truth? In fact, this was preposterous. Who had ever heard of a prince disguised as a frog? And even if there should be a prince under there, why was she the one who had to give the kiss? It was a lot safer not to get involved.

"But then the princess began to consider the situation more carefully—*what if there really were a handsome prince under all that ugly green skin? What if he really were telling the truth? Just because she had never encountered this before did not mean that it wasn't possible. And why not she to be the deliverer of the kiss? It might actually be exciting to be involved, a whole new adventure.*"

John laughed as he continued, "What did she do? She took a chance! She trusted her positive instincts. She kissed that frog, and the handsome prince appeared. And they lived happily ever after."

John was smiling. "Now," he chuckled, "I go through that whole story for this one reason. And that is so you will remember that our job is to become frog-kissers!"

John leaned back and smiled broadly. The man had to smile, too.

"A frog-kisser? What does that mean?"

"What do you think it means?" asked John.

"I haven't the slightest idea," replied the man candidly.

John looked at the man. "What we are talking about, my friend, is love—nonjudgmental, unconditional love. And the truth is, that kind of love conquers cancer!"

"Love?" asked the man. "Is that where the journey leads?"

"It certainly does," said John. "It's what frog-kissing is all about."

"What do you mean?" said the man.

"If I could give you just one piece of advice on how to

Nonjudgmental,

Unconditional

Love

Conquers

Cancer.

conquer cancer," said John, "it would be to love, to be a frog-kisser. And my advice would be to love yourself first—to kiss the frog in the mirror.

"The Cancer Conqueror teaches that many people, particularly many cancer patients, grow up with the idea that they are somehow flawed and that this lack of perfection in some way makes them unacceptable. People who feel like this often act as if they must cover up this central defect if they are to be accepted, if they are to have any chance for love.

"Feeling unloved and feeling as if they are not worthy of love, these people, to greater and lesser degrees, retreat into isolation and loneliness. This retreat is a natural outcome of hiding their fear of another person's discovering that inner deficiency that makes them feel so unworthy.

"The Cancer Conqueror cites how often cancer patients tend to be perfectionistic, overachieving workaholics who repress their real feelings. They judge themselves by their work—how well they did it, how much they did of it, and how long they worked at it. And these same people often don't feel good about their accomplishments. They may even resent others for not noticing their work."

The man raised his hand to stop John. "That's me, a perfectionistic, overachieving workaholic! And nobody *ever* appreciates what I've done!"

"There are some heavy prices for living life by those beliefs," said John. "It's back to that whole thought of a central defect again. These people want to be judged by what they *do*—their work—rather than who they are as a person. And the trouble is, their good work is never good enough. And the praise, from self and others, is never quite loud enough!"

"Oh wow!" exclaimed the man. "You've just described me."

"Does this behavior often lead you to feelings of emptiness and disappointment?" asked John.

"Constantly," he nodded.

"Because of the profound inner emptiness and the despair, people with this characteristic often come to view all their relationships in terms of finding something to fill the void. This is the conditional love you hear so much about. These people give love, give of themselves, give anything, only on the condition that they get something in return for it."

"Like what?" asked the man.

"It could be anything. People's conditions for love can be vastly different. Some people want economic security. Others want love and nurturing in return. Many people seek approval from others. But there are patterns, a few common threads running through each one.

"The trouble with behavior that places conditions on love is that it is manipulative. It is conditional, contingent upon getting something back. It is an 'if' love. It leads to an even deeper sense of emptiness because it will always fail."

"If the conditions are being met, it wouldn't fail. It would work just fine," contended the man.

"Not for long," insisted John. "We're talking about human beings, people with expectations that escalate. It is just a matter of time before either the expectations are not met, or the people trying to fulfill those expectations come to see themselves as being manipulated and quit. But that's only the first level.

"On a deeper level, this 'if love' prevents the person from understanding his or her true and unique self. If you are always spending energy determining the degree to which your expectations are being met, and the degree of love which you will return, you'll never be able to understand the *true you*. You'll never be able to hear your own music. It is a vicious circle that results in perpetual disappointment, deepening emptiness, and personal despair."

"Are you saying that I love conditionally?" asked the man.

"Yes. I do, you do, we all do," answered John. "At sometime in our life, we all love with 'ifs.' The trouble is, it doesn't stop there. That despair born of loneliness often leads to something even more insidious—judgmentalism.

"These are the ones who are consistently critical of people and circumstances that are different from their own views. The Cancer Conqueror points out that many people were brought up with a lot of 'shoulds,' 'oughts,' and 'have-tos': *A woman should be at home. A man ought to be a good provider. Children have to eat all their dinner.* There are literally hundreds of these learned rules.

"Those who are judgmental get into a pattern where other people's worth is measured by how closely they conform to the judgmental person's rules.

"Everything gets judged. Everyone is labeled as flawed and no good. All this is an attempt on the part of the judgmental to build themselves up while tearing others down. The vicious circle continues—disappointment, emptiness, and despair."

"This is really depressing," said the man. "I thought we were going to talk about LIVE."

John smiled, "We are. We're going to talk about how to LIVE by loving. But to do that, we need this perspective on judgmental and conditional love. The Cancer Conqueror once traced how crucial unconditional love really is. He believes that all disease has a lack of love as its roots.

"He explained how love that is judgmental and conditional leads to depression and thus allows physical vulnerability. He even went so far as to say that he felt all

Healing

Has At

Its Roots

The Ability

To Give

And

Receive

Nonjudgmental,

Unconditional

Love.

healing has at its roots the ability to give and receive nonjudgmental, unconditional love."

"What does this mean?" asked the man.

"It means that our task becomes learning to give and receive nonjudgmental, unconditional love. It means to stop judging. The Cancer Conqueror put this in an unforgettable, clear perspective when he talked about three valid standards to judge by. He feels there are moral standards, legal standards, and law-of-nature standards.

"Perhaps an example would help. Let's say friends with whom you have an appointment are late. Your reaction includes thoughts of anger. 'They don't respect my time. They are always late. They make me mad. They're really not considerate people.' There is a lot of judging going on here.

"But there is another choice. We could re-evaluate our thoughts about the lateness in light of the three standards. Does their lateness break any moral law? Is this in the same class as murdering someone or intentionally harming someone? Does their lateness break any legal standard? Is this behavior in the same class as speeding at a hundred miles per hour? And does the friend's lateness go against any natural law? Is the behavior in the same category as chlorofluorocarbons damaging the ozone?"

"Okay," chuckled the man. "Those are pretty exaggerated examples."

"Not really. Those are just the type of thoughts that trigger judging all the time. The point is that if someone's behavior doesn't break a moral, legal, or natural law, forget it! Don't judge it! If we can just release ourselves from judgmental behavior, we'll be a long way down the road toward learning how to love. And when we add unconditional love—loving without expecting anything in return—to nonjudgmental behavior, the two work together to form a powerful basis for living.

"I am convinced that the energy we have put into judging and into expectations can be redirected to help us get well. In that sense, unconditional, nonjudgmental love is a powerful stimulant to our natural immune systems. In that sense, love is not merely emotional. It is physiological. In a real sense, love can always conquer cancer and often cures it, too!"

John stopped as the man finished his notes. "It all relates to another facet of frog-kissing, acceptance versus approval. It's the difference between accepting people for who they are versus approving of them for what they do, their behavior. This applies not only to how you relate to others, but it especially applies to how you see yourself.

"For example, you must keep in mind that you are more than your behavior. You have great worth *outside* your behavior. You have worth as a person, as a living human being in addition to what you may do and even in spite of what you may do! The key is to truly learn to accept your worth as a person even though you may not approve of your behavior."

The man was silent, deep in thought. Finally, in a whisper, he said, "Tell me more."

"Okay," said John, "let's go from looking within to looking without. Let's examine other people. They are just the same as you and me. Their worth isn't wrapped up in what they do. We can learn to accept others as fellow citizens of the world even though we may not approve of their behavior. My task is to *accept* others, not *approve* of others."

"Accepting and not approving removes me from having to be the judge, doesn't it?" asked the man.

"That's it," John agreed enthusiastically. "That's precisely it. See, when we judge, we don't really see the other person, or ourselves, as whole people. Most of us were brought up in an environment where the emphasis was

My Task
Is To
Accept
Others,

Not
Approve
Of Others.

placed on constructive criticism. This is usually a disguise for faultfinding. When we judge, we find fault and then almost invariably label that person, or ourselves, as unworthy. We assume the other person to be wholly bad. We assume ourselves to be wholly unworthy. "But if we can separate persons from their behavior, there is much to lovingly accept. We can go from being faultfinders to becoming lovefinders! Only then can we hear that strong inner voice saying, 'I love you and accept you just as you are.'"

The man was again silent. This was new. And somewhat frightening.

If you decided to love, you left yourself vulnerable. People could take advantage of that love.

"Can't other people take advantage of that love?" asked the man, voicing his doubts. "Can't they take advantage of you?"

"Only if you have expectations about extending that love," said John. "Remember, our job is to love unconditionally. The person's reaction makes little difference.

"Perhaps the classic example is the case of the diners who go into a fashionable restaurant for dinner. They find the service deplorable and the waitress unfriendly and rude. Feeling angry and mistreated, the diners feel justified in their grievance and hostility and leave the waitress no tip.

"Now let's replay the scene from the start. This time let's assume that the patrons discover, just as they sit down, that the husband of the waitress died two days ago and that she has five children at home who are solely dependent on her for support.

"This changes everything. The customers adopt a new role that overlooks the behavior as threatening and sees the waitress as fearful, recognizing that she is calling out for love and acceptance. Their response accepts her as a person without having to approve of her actions and be-havior. Their attitude is now loving, a response which they demonstrate by leaving an extra large tip.

"Do you grasp this?" asked John. "The scene was the same in each case. The characters were the same. The place was the same. The words were the same. However, in the first scene, the events were seen through the window of approval, with conditional love. And in the second, they were seen through the window of accept-ance—nonjudgmental, unconditional love.

"What changed was the patrons' role. Nothing else. They went from faultfinding to lovefinding. We can live life this way! We can conquer cancer this way!"

The man was reflective. "Is this . . . frog-kissing?" he asked.

"Wonderful!" shouted John. "You've got it! That's it!"

Again the man was quiet and thoughtful. The idea had many implications. "This extends to other areas of life, doesn't it?" asked the man.

"It surely does," smiled John. "Frog-kissing has unlim-ited applications! Some people feel they are *married* to a frog! Some think they *work* for a frog. Some people see everybody else in the world as a frog."

Both men laughed.

"But those are just the windows of approval, judgment, and expectation that guarantee we will never know the power of love. Realize that other people do not have to change for me to love them. Instead, *I* have to change for me to love them! Isn't that a revolutionary thought?"

John jumped to his feet and waved his arms, "Our first job is to go from faultfinder to lovefinder—of ourselves and of others. And only we can make that choice. It de-pends on us! It's within our control. Isn't that wonderful? Isn't that a happy, hopeful thought?"

The man smiled. You just had to feel joy to see John

Other People
Do Not Have
To Change
For
Me To Love
Them —

I Have To
Change
For
Me To
Love Them.

wave his arms exuberantly and talk about love in his pleasant big voice. And he had to admit, there *was* hope in this frog-kissing message. How refreshing—within us there was wholeness, not some central defect. And outside us there were others whom we could choose to accept even though we may not approve. We didn't have to judge everyone! Going from faultfinder to lovefinder—this was *good!*

"There's a happiness in this outlook, isn't there?" asked the man. "Frog-kissing leads to joy, doesn't it?"

"You're great!" said John. "I can see you're going to conquer your cancer because you're so open to these principles. You've already grasped the next step in LIVE—joy! With love there comes happiness. And with happiness, joy is possible.

"You know, inside each of us is a child—the good, non-manipulative, fun-loving, filled-with-joy little person who needs to be nourished. It is the belief of the Cancer Conqueror that most cancer patients don't nourish this inner child. And by not honoring the child's real needs, they may be contributing to their illness or inhibiting their recovery.

"I used to deny the needs of my child," said John. "I always felt that those needs were far behind me. After all, I had matured. I had grown. I didn't need to laugh and play. Or so I thought. Wow, was I wrong! My needs to honor my inner child are very strong. I'll bet you have that same need."

The man said, "I'm not sure what you're talking about. Tell me more."

"There are two parts of finding joy. The first is an attitude issue. To me, joy is giving life a big hug, embracing all the beauty and wonder and goodness there is in this world. Joy is not how much you possess, but how much you enjoy.

Joy
Is Not
How Much
You Possess,

But
How Much
You
Enjoy.

"I once saw a bumper sticker that said, 'The one with the most toys wins!' My suggestion is that 'the one with the most *joys* wins.'

"It is that attitude that looks for joy in the small, precious packages and makes the most of them, knowing that the big packages of joy are really few and far between."

"That's joy!" said the man. "It sounds wonderful. I wish I were able to capture more of those moments."

"You can," said John. "You see, the second part of finding joy, of letting the inner child come out, is action. Simply put, we need to allow time for play."

"Play?" questioned the man.

"Yes, play," smiled John. "The kid inside needs time to play every day."

"But play sounds so . . . so . . . I guess it feels childish," said the man.

"That's the idea!" retorted John. "That's just what we're looking for—ways to nurture that inner child. This can really be an important step in your journey.

"The idea is to have fun, to create an enjoyable experience. The person who can find joy and laugh will be much better off than the stoic person who seldom cracks a smile and won't acknowledge his or her feelings.

"That's what you saw me doing as you walked in today. That juggling is one of my forms of play. And far from taking away from my capacity for work, it actually helps increase my energy for living.

"When I first heard the Cancer Conqueror talk about laughter and play, I, too, assumed it wasn't for me. I possessed a certain rigidity about releasing the inner child. Then the Cancer Conqueror talked about messages we may have learned as children. His ideas really hit home.

"Early on in life I was conditioned to 'try hard,' 'be serious,' 'be strong,' 'be successful,' 'be a good provider.' And I have heard women describe their messages of 'be

Play

Is

Okay.

perfect,' 'please everybody,' 'nurture everyone,' 'look nice.' When I realized how I had been conditioned, I actually had to start out by giving myself an assignment. I had to schedule time to play. Isn't that crazy?" The man shook his head. "No, not at all. This cancer journey has once again confronted me with me. That's exactly the way I am. I learned the same things. I have the same attitudes toward play that you did."

"I hear you being a little tough on yourself," said John. "Instead, just decide to re-parent yourself on this one. First, I gave myself permission to play. I made play a more important part of my life. I used to say, 'I'll play after work.' Well, the work is never done. Now I let myself treat work and play with the same attitude—both are important. Both deserve my best. I had to decide that play is okay.

"The next thing I did was really helpful. I gave my inner child a name! As a youngster, nobody called me 'John.' I was known by my nickname, 'Buddy.' I always liked that. So I started calling my inner child 'Buddy'!

"It's great! I still do it! At first I asked what my inner child needed to *get* well. And today I ask Buddy what he needs to *stay* well.

"A helpful perspective for me was when the Cancer Conqueror suggested that we think of the part of us that got cancer as this inner child. Then our task becomes centered on taking care of that child, nurturing the child back to health, helping the child conquer cancer.

"So when I ask Buddy what he needs to stay well, I'm trying to get in touch with myself attitudinally, emotionally, and behaviorally on a very basic level. Buddy invariably wants me to honor his needs to experience laughter, play, and joy. And I listen. I now honor those needs," smiled John.

"That's neat how you talk with your inner child. I'm

*What Does
My
Inner Child
Need
To Get
Well?*

going to do that today!" said the man. "I've often sensed some of these things, but I never really talked to my child. This sounds exciting."

"When you talk to your inner child," said John, "you might want to do what the Cancer Conqueror suggests. He had me write out fifty different things I could do, actual activities I felt would bring me fun and produce joy in my life. Just try that exercise. It was very difficult for me to find fifty items at first. I suppose my child was so undernourished that he had forgotten how to play. But now my list has more than 150 activities—and it's still increasing."

"That's wonderful," said the man. "But I think I'm going to have trouble coming up with even ten ways to play."

"You'll learn," said John. "I found that it was important for me just to block the time to play. In the beginning there were some days that I didn't do a thing. But just scheduling the time, taking the time, was helpful. And soon I began to fill that time with activities.

"Once I heard the Cancer Conqueror talk about play in conjunction with treatments. A woman dreaded going in for treatments. So the Cancer Conqueror had her sandwich the treatments between play. Before she went in, she scheduled thirty minutes of piano playing for herself. And afterwards, she went window shopping, just to treat herself to the sights and senses there. Interesting. Her dread of the treatments decreased, and the side effects she was experiencing completely disappeared. She was now taking care of her inner child.

"So nurture your inner child," continued John. "Play is much more than an activity; it is an attitude that generates energy for healing. And we're never too tired to play. If we think that, perhaps that's a signal that we need play the most. Honor your inner child's needs."

"Thank you for giving me permission to do so," said the man. And he chuckled out loud. "You know, I already feel better. Just the idea of letting myself play is wonderful. And the idea of frog-kissing, maybe that's even better! I'm going to become a playful frog-kisser! How about that?"

Both men laughed out loud! Perhaps it was the mental picture that a playful frog-kisser conjured up. At any rate there was significant release in their laughter—a safety valve was being opened.

Then John spoke again. "It's wonderful to see you laugh, to see you smile and express that joy in your eyes. Yet as great as being a playful frog-kisser might be, there's something even better."

"What is it?" asked the man.

"Well, all the love in the world, all the joy in the world, resolving all our problems, even changing all our beliefs are empty without one essential ingredient.

"I once heard a person describe it this way, 'All our efforts are like a long string of zeros. They mean nothing without a digit in front of them. That digit is peace of mind.'"

The man was quiet, reflecting on what he had just heard.

"Inner peace is really the central message of the Cancer Conqueror. The goal is to have peace of mind, not just to cure cancer.

"Personal peace creates an environment conducive to healing within the body. It is perhaps the best way to allow the body's own healing mechanisms to function."

"Okay," said the man, "I like what you're saying, but really what is personal peace? And how do I go about achieving it?"

"Good questions," said John. "I like the definition the Cancer Conqueror teaches: 'Personal peace is

The Goal
Is To Have
Peace Of Mind —

Not
Just To
Cure Cancer.

transcending oneself in order to nurture inner harmony.'
Let's give this definition a closer look.

"First, personal peace is transcending. The idea is that
personal peace is intent, choice, and action. It is not some
chance occurrence. And personal peace transcends self—
meaning that the decision is made to consciously set aside
self-limitations of fear, anger, and guilt and to reach
for the serene greatness that rests within each of us. And
peace of mind is inner harmony, inner contentment, inner
tranquillity. There is the definition. There is our goal."

"I don't hear you talking about outer quietness," said
the man.

"Many people would include that," said John, "and
others would not. For me, personal peace includes times
of outer quietness as well as times of activity. The Cancer
Conqueror really takes peace out of the activity realm
when he says, 'You will know personal peace when what
you think, what you say, and what you do are essentially
consistent.' I believe this is what we're really after—
inner consistency. Quietness may be a part of that. But
activity may also have a part.

"You see, it isn't so much the physical aspects as it is
the inner aspects, the emotional components, that make
for personal peace. This is especially important for the
cancer patient. Realize that peace of mind is independent
from our physical condition."

There was a pause. "Ah-ha," said the man. "A light
bulb has just gone on in my mind. Personal peace really
brings it all together, doesn't it?"

John nodded his agreement.

"How do I achieve this peace? How do I work to make
this a way of life?"

John stood, stretched, and walked across the office.
"You know," he began, "of all the changes the Cancer
Conqueror encouraged me to make, the daily pursuit of

Peace
Of Mind
Is
Independent
From Our
Physical
Condition.

personal peace has had the single most dramatic effect on my outer and inner life. If there were one change I had to point to which most altered my daily schedule, one which had the most potential for healing, it would be this pursuit—this acceptance of the profound personal peace that is available to all of us."

"I'm not sure I understand," said the man.

"I practice daily quiet time, a daily dose of tranquility, that gets me in touch with the deeper levels of personal peace that are always waiting there for me to enjoy."

The man looked a bit puzzled. "This seems a little far out. What do you mean?"

John smiled that reassuring grin as he sat down. "Just listen with your mind. There is so much healing potential here.

"Twice each day, I set aside fifteen minutes to calm my mind, to examine my spirit, and to affirm my total wellness in all areas of my life. Here at work, at home, when I travel, wherever I am, I find or make a quiet spot where I won't be disturbed. Twice each day—more if I am dealing with a lot of stress—I still my spirit, affirm myself, and find personal peace.

"I sit in a comfortable position, close my eyes and turn my attention to my muscles. I take special care first to tense and then to relax my muscles from head to feet, particularly those in the shoulder, neck, and forehead. In fact, one of my biggest muscle tension problems was my jaw—I was always clenching it, gritting my teeth, and pushing my tongue up against the roof of my mouth. No wonder I was always getting headaches. From the shoulders up, I was one knot of tense muscles. I now take time to consciously relax this area.

"Next, I conceive of my mind as the surface of a body of water. I have the mental picture of a lake. And when I think of the stress and tension that may have been part of my day, I see the surface of the lake churning with whitecaps.

"But then I imagine changing that scene, having the power to make those waves dissipate. I make the lake's undulating surface calm—placid and smooth, just like a mirror. At the same time I will repeat the word *peace* silently in time with my breathing.

"Amazingly, not only does my mind follow with thoughts that are calming and soothing, but my whole spirit feels a weight lifted. When a stressful thought or worry comes to mind, I gently dismiss it and make my thoughts go right back to the calm smooth surface of that lake and to my focus word *peace.*"

The man smiled, "I have to admit that just hearing you describe your daily dose of quiet is peaceful."

"Wonderful," said John. "That tells me you can easily and effectively do this exercise. Remember, the goal is first to relax the muscles. This, in itself, is a healing experience and will help in your total wellness. Then calm the mind. Dismiss thoughts that come and return to the placid, peaceful surface of the lake."

John continued, "I also use this as an opportunity to examine my spirit and to listen to the deeper messages of harmony found in quieting the mind. This relates to the resolve process.

"Many thoughts that cross my mind in my internal dialogue have to do with judging and with my feeling that I have to be right. When I observe my spirit and ask if those positions are bringing me love, peace, and joy, invariably it is a revealing and growing experience.

"I listen to my inner self. Some call this intuition. Others call it conscience, inner wisdom, or the subconscious. I just think of it as my inner self.

"I ask questions like, 'Am I experiencing love, joy, and peace?' Then I wait for my inner self to respond. 'Is my marriage reflecting love, joy, and peace?' 'What about my work? My physical condition? Our social life? Our finances?' The idea is to examine the important areas of life and then listen to the inner self evaluate.

"When I get a positive response, I'm thankful for it. I express gratitude. When I hear a negative response, I ask, 'What is the message here? How do I need to change?' Then I listen for direction from within.

"With practice, I was able to get on speaking terms with myself. I now feel strong inner guidance is an important part of my life."

"How do you know you're not just selfishly coming up with the answers you want to hear?" asked the man.

"Excellent question. You see, I truly believe that love, joy, and peace are my aim and what is best for my life. Love, joy, and peace are what is important. If I receive signals that are based in fear, anger, and guilt, I know I need to change. I need to let go again. If I receive answers based on love, joy, and peace, I trust them because they are consistent with my aim."

"But when you say, 'Let go,' what do you mean?" pondered the man.

"You've asked a profound question that has been asked through the ages. To me," continued John, "letting go means adopting an attitude of relaxed trust. Relaxed trust is that sense of inner harmony—that serenity, that contentment—which comes from knowing all is well, even if you have cancer.

"You *can* let go. You don't have to judge. You don't have to approve. You don't have to control. You don't have to be right every time. You can give yourself a vacation from trying to be Manager of the Universe! That's letting go."

Both men laughed. How often they both had tried to assume those roles and take those positions. New thinking was required. "Examining, observing, listening—those are keys to a better way."

John continued, "And this leads to the final part of my daily quiet time—affirming myself. Many people use affirmations to replace old ingrained thinking patterns. Positive phrases, repeated often and with emotion, can lead to new understanding. They help counter conditioned thinking. Affirmations can help change our beliefs about cancer. The end of your quiet time is an appropriate time for these affirmations.

"But there is another side to affirming. This has to do with affirming—some would say directing, others might say rehearsing—your body's own built-in healing capabilities.

"The idea of mental reviews of desired activities is well accepted. Olympic athletes have used this creative imagination to gain a competitive edge. For example, the more an athlete imagines a successful jump over the crossbar, the more deeply etched the mental and emotional circuits become. In short, we become what we think about."

"Exactly what are you suggesting?" questioned the man.

John looked the man squarely in the eyes. "I am suggesting that you have significant control over your immune system, your natural defense against cancer."

"Is this more of the psychoneuroimmunology I have previously learned about?" asked the man.

"It is," said John. "And the primary technique for purposely stimulating our immune system is using creative imagination during our daily quiet time.

"One researcher called it healing with brain chemistry. Our immune defenses tend to weaken under stress. Quiet time with relaxation exercises and creative imagination may be one way to control the bio-chemical stress triggers and thus keep our resistance up."

"Do I hear you saying that in addition to my emotions influencing my immune system, I can also consciously enhance the functioning of my immune system?"

John spoke firmly and with deep conviction, "I am saying that creatively and consciously imagining our immune system functioning effectively may indeed enhance it. I am also recognizing that the immune system may be positively triggered as the roadblocks of fear, anger, and guilt are replaced with love, joy, and peace. And I am suggesting that as we imagine malignant cells being eliminated, and as we imagine ourselves as healthy, whole and feeling well, our entire being—body, mind, and spirit—will move in the direction of health. That is something we cherish! That is what we're striving for!"

"I've heard of this before," said the man. "In fact, I'm afraid I recently read that some doctors think the whole thing is self-deception."

"I'm sorry you read that," said John. "Instead of taking that article at face value, would you try an experiment with me here and now? Would you be willing to see if we could get our thoughts to trigger a system in our body?"

"Sure, I'm willing to do that. What do we do?"

John got comfortable, reclining slightly in his chair and stretching his legs out. He invited the man to do the same. "Okay, now just close your eyes and imagine yourself in your kitchen. Go over to the refrigerator and take out a big, yellow lemon that is in there. As you hold the bright, firm lemon, feel the texture of its skin. Feel the shape. See the color. Lift it to your nose and smell its sharp pungent odor. Now walk over to the counter where you find a paring knife. Cut the lemon in half. Notice the spray and smell the aroma as the juice runs over your fingers. Now take one of the halves and put it between your teeth. Bite hard and savor the juices as they roll over your tongue and throughout your mouth."

"Okay! Okay!" laughed the man. "You've made your point. I can't believe the amount of saliva that produces!"

"The fact is," said John, "the body cannot tell the difference between what is actually taking place and what you are *imagining* is taking place. This principle is at the very heart of what I was saying about the vital importance of imagining our immune systems functioning effectively. Does this example do anything to shift your thinking about this being some sort of deception?"

"Well, I have visualized many times before. I used it in my work. I know it works there. And I see no reason why it wouldn't work here."

John smiled. "That's it. You see, we have to protect our belief. Just one article that is negative, particularly if it is written by some authority figure like a doctor, can close the door on all sorts of possibilities. Let's learn to honor our own beliefs and respond to our own judgment."

"How did you go about enhancing your immune system?" said the man.

"My method was to see my cancer as something weak, and my immune system as something strong that would easily have the ability to handle the cancer. And during my treatment period, I imagined the chemotherapy as strong, a strong friend who was there to help rid my body of cancer."

"Yes, but how did you know what a cancer cell looks like? And the same for your immune system and the treatment?"

John gave a chuckle before he began. "You know what I did? I gave them all symbols. I didn't actually know what they technically looked like. I was told that wasn't important. It wasn't even critical that I knew where the cancer was located. What was important is that I imagined my immune system and treatment as being effective.

"So I imagined my cancer as ice cubes. And I saw my immune system as hot water. I viewed chemotherapy as an intense ray of white-hot light. The hot water and the ray of light melted the ice and the cancer was flushed from my body naturally. I felt this was a very effective image for me. Others have used the Pac-man game as something powerful for an immune system image. Still others that are frequently used include big fish that eat smaller fish, soldiers that defeat a weak opponent, or images of a similar nature.

"Just choose a weak image for the cancer and strong images for both your immune system and your treatment. And 'see' the dead cancer cells flushed from the body normally and naturally. Then end your quiet time by affirming yourself as healthy and free from cancer.

"This isn't self-deception. It is self-direction. And it moves us in the direction of wellness. What do you think about using your creative imagination?" asked John.

"Well, I think it is something I'm going to try. I can't help but believe in its potential. I've seen the principle work in other areas of my life. So I'm going to put it to use here."

"There's one more important thing that needs to be said," John added. "Creative imagination and affirming our own healing capabilities are different from quieting our minds and examining our spirits. Creative imagination is goal-directed. We actively guide our imagination. Quieting our minds and examining our spirits are observation-directed. They help us become more aware of thoughts and choices. They aid us in deciding to let go of those things that hold us back."

"Which is more important?" asked the man.

"Realize that we aren't simply imagining white blood cells attacking cancer cells. Instead, we are moving our entire being—body, mind, and spirit—in the direction of

We Are

Moving

Our Entire Being —

Body, Mind, and Spirit —

In The Direction

Of Wellness.

wellness. And this is a direction demonstrated by love, joy, and peace.

"I am suggesting that as important as your creative imagination can be, consider it as an adjunct to the main purpose of your daily quiet times. I suggest that you keep as your main goals quieting the mind and examining the spirit. The new awareness that they can bring is really what you are after. They generate peace of mind!"

The man finished his notes. "We've covered a lot of material."

John smiled that special smile once again.

"We have! But that's it, my friend. That's LIVE. Love, joy, and peace. To be a peaceful, playful frog-kisser! That's the goal. And it's also the essence of health!"

"That's a lot," said the man. "Can you help me summarize the points before I leave?"

"You've taken good notes," said John. "You can review them on your own. But write this down. It's the Cancer Conqueror's one sentence summary of LIVE:

To LIVE means to move our lives toward our own unique experience of love, joy, and peace.

"Spend time contemplating the special meaning of that for you."

The men stood. John put his hands on the man's shoulders and looked straight into his eyes. "Now go and live your life one day at a time. You can never tell when the greatest moment of your life is going to happen to you. So go and live each moment as if it were the greatest—the greatest for love, for joy, and for peace."

The men embraced. "Thank you," said the man. He left feeling at peace with himself and the world.

As soon as the man was home, he sat at his desk and summarized his notes.

LIVE SUMMARY

1. Nonjudgmental, unconditional love conquers cancer.
2. Healing has at its roots the ability to give and receive nonjudgmental, unconditional love.
3. My task is to accept others, not approve of others.
4. Other people do not have to change for me to love them; I have to change for me to love them.
5. Joy is not how much you possess, but how much you enjoy.
6. Play is okay. Make my list of fifty activities that are fun, that bring me joy.
7. Recognize and talk to my inner child. Ask, "What do you need to get well?"
8. The goal is to have peace of mind, not just to cure cancer. Peace of mind creates an environment conducive to healing the body.
9. Peace of mind is independent from my physical condition.
10. Schedule daily quiet time—at least fifteen minutes twice a day.
    — focus thoughts on a peaceful scene, dismissing other thoughts as they come and returning to that peaceful place.
    — listen to my inner self, being thankful for love, joy, and peace and being open to messages to change.
    — affirm myself and affirm my own immune system working to overcome the cancer.

SECTION 6

The Cancer Conqueror Explains

The man felt good. John's LIVE message had given him hope! He called the Cancer Conqueror the very next morning.

"I have completed the assignment," he said. They scheduled a meeting that afternoon, right after the man's appointment with his doctor.

When the man arrived at the Cancer Conqueror's home, his mood had changed. The Cancer Conqueror picked up on the change immediately. "Compared to our phone call this morning, you seem troubled. Do you need to talk?"

"Yes, I do, and I'll tell you exactly what it is," said the man. I've just come from my oncologist's office. And while I'm doing great, just seeing all those patients in that waiting room wasn't a good experience. It's depressing! I talked with a woman who had just had a recurrence. It's a frightening prospect to work at getting well only to have the cancer return."

"Wait! Slow down!" said the Cancer Conqueror. "You're *awfulizing*, you're letting your thoughts assume the worst possible outcomes.

"Admittedly, an oncology office is not the best place to seek a lift. You see people there who are hurting, who are feeling hopeless and overwhelmed. When I need to schedule an appointment with my oncologist, I first become aware that I'll need to toughen myself mentally. And one of the issues is the people in that waiting room. I'm probably going to see some emaciated folks with fear and depression written all over their faces. Just looking at them can cause me to question myself and my own beliefs.

"But realizing this is helpful. If I am feeling strong emotionally, I often make an effort to sit by someone who looks especially needy. My goal is then to give whatever word of encouragement I can honestly muster. I try to take a negative and turn it into something positive. And when I do, invariably I feel better for having done so."

"Okay," said the man. "I understand what you're suggesting. But the fact is, I talked to a woman who had been cancer-free for seven years. Now it is back! The idea of a recurrence always haunting me is really frightening."

The Cancer Conqueror was firm. "The fact is, the possibility of recurrence will always be with you. The course of the disease is uncertain. Even so, there is reason for hope.

"There is a pervasive belief that is behind almost all worries of recurrence. The belief goes something like, 'Yes, you may battle the cancer with some success, but in the end the biological process will win and it will eventually get you.' Have you ever heard that?"

"Sure, just today I heard that from the woman who had the recurrence."

"That belief is a major untruth. It is reasonably common for people to go into remission, have a recurrence, and eventually enjoy recovery. Once again, the importance of our beliefs comes into play. We must first understand that recurrence does not mean imminent death.

"Yet, we need to treat recurrence as a crisis. For some, this is obvious. Their pain is significant, or perhaps they can actually feel growth. And it is common for fear to be

Recurrence
Does Not
Mean
Imminent
Death.

more intense with recurrence. They may also feel out of
control and lose faith in their medical team, their treatment, as well as the program they have been studying.
Feelings like 'I've failed; I give up' are common. That's
probably what you saw this morning with that lady."

"That was precisely it," said the man. "And it scares
me."

"I've gone through recurrence," said the Cancer Conqueror. "It was frightening. But I did some things that
made it a turning point. Consider these. First, I treated
myself very gently. I had been back at work, but now I
took more time off. I scheduled a vacation at one of our
favorite places. And I spent time alone, time to reflect.

"I talked with others, people who had overcome the
illness. It was helpful to understand that most of them
had also gone through recurrence. Almost all had used
recurrence as a time to reevaluate.

"So I followed their advice. I went back to the medical
team and had the doctors review the recent evaluations
in detail and answer my questions. This helped.

"Then I went back over my beliefs, examined the major
emotional stresses I needed to resolve, and looked more
closely at what personal needs weren't being met.

"Finally, I asked a tough question of myself. Did I want
to work toward health once again or did I want to accept
death and spend my energy preparing for it?

"You can see which I chose—I was willing once again
to work toward recovery."

"But what if you had died? There weren't any guarantees that you would recover," said the man.

"Not one," said the Cancer Conqueror. "But guarantees
aren't the issue. I said I would work toward recovery, that
I would work toward health. I couldn't guarantee recovery or health. No one could. I could only work toward
them. I had to realize that even though I didn't control

Even Though
I Don't
Control
My Destiny,

I Do
Influence
My Destiny.

my destiny, I did influence it. And I chose to influence it toward health."

The man finished his notes and looked up. "I need something with more certainty. I am expecting this program to bring me health."

"It can," said the Cancer Conqueror. "But are you also saying that you'll reject it if it doesn't meet all your expectations? I can't give you any guarantee. I can only share that for me it was—and is—a hill-and-valley experience.

"I refused to view the valley of recurrence as a failure. Instead, I again chose to view recurrence as a message. I needed once again to understand the message and decide what my response would be.

"For me the message of recurrence was clearly that I was not taking care of myself as I needed to. Up to that time, I was not really following the diet I knew was best for me, I was exercising only occasionally, I wasn't taking time to play, I only sporadically worked with my creative imagination, and I had only partially resolved some of the emotional conflict issues.

"When I honestly looked at myself, I realized that I had, in many ways, returned to the lifestyle that contributed to my initial illness. After I realized this, I came to believe that recurrence was my body's way of telling me to choose to change once again—to work toward health or to accept death and begin that process."

The man was uneasy. "Maybe the real issue of recurrence with me is the possibility that death is near. That scares me so much. I don't want to die. It's all so frightening."

"Okay," said the Cancer Conqueror. "Let's talk about death. When you think about death, what is it that you fear?"

"Oh, wow," said the man pensively. "The whole thing is frightening. I don't even like to think about it. Maybe it's the fear of lying there helpless, not being able to take care of myself. I don't want to be an invalid. And the people we leave behind. That's sad. And it's also this emptiness about no longer existing. I get depressed just thinking that it's all going to come to an end. I hate to talk about death."

"Then let's face this fear," said the Cancer Conqueror. "Instead of saying we don't want to deal with an issue, let's just take fear of death and start to conquer it right now.

"You said you feared three things about death. One was the issue of being an invalid. That has to do with the process of dying, the quality of death. And you also said you felt sad about leaving. That has to do with severing our earthly ties. Finally you said you felt empty about no longer existing. This is the issue of what may or may not come after death."

"Yes," sighed the man. "That's it."

"There is much we could say about death," said the Cancer Conqueror.

"Much has been written about it. I encourage you to seek out the resources you need to handle this issue. So today, let's not make it our aim to fully explore death. Instead, let's just attempt to help you through the basic issue of facing your own fear of death.

"I remember discussing the issue of death with a pastor. In a blinding flash of the obvious he said, 'First, I assume you believe you will die. I mean, the statistics are overwhelming! A thousand out of a thousand people die! There don't seem to be many exceptions! Life in that body will end someday.'

"The implications of his humor hit me immediately. Of course I would die. The question wasn't 'if'; the question was 'when' and 'how.'

"Many cancer patients are anxious about death's

'when' and 'how.' There is sadness and possibly anger over the prospect of a shortened life—the when. Perhaps there are dreams still to pursue and people still to love. So the thought of shortening the lifespan seems unfair.

"Yet in a real sense, people live on in the memories of others. If we want to guarantee a loving memory, if we want to guarantee that we accomplished something great with our lives, then we need to love, and love now! That's the secret to overcoming the fear of death's 'when'—it's to love now, today, this hour, while we have the opportunity. A life's value is not measured by its duration but by its donations of love!"

"That's helpful," said the man. "Very helpful."

"And then there is the dread of a low quality of death. A long, debilitating illness that could drain the family and the patient emotionally and financially is the real fear. This is the unpleasant 'how' part, a fear that there is little control over death.

"Unlike many causes of death, cancer usually allows ample time to prepare. This preparation, this taking control can be very comforting. Some may want to plan their funeral. Others may want to sign a living will which instructs doctors to discontinue life-support systems when there appears to be no hope of survival. Normally there is time to prepare wills and put estates in order.

"All these things can be done to gain some control over death. And there's even more control. It's amazing. A study of several thousand deaths showed that almost 50 percent occurred within three months after people's birthdays, while fewer than 10 percent came in the three months prior to their birthdays."

"I don't understand the point," said the man.

"Just this," said the Cancer Conqueror. "People seem to have an influence over the time of death. Many

A

Life's Value

Is Not

Measured

By Its

Duration

But

By Its

Donations

Of Love.

'postponed' their death until after they had celebrated their birthday."

"That's incredible," said the man. "Can we be certain?"

"No," said the Cancer Conqueror, "there isn't a certainty here. I'm not saying that we can live as long as we want. But I am suggesting that we do have some degree of control that perhaps we once thought did not exist."

The Cancer Conqueror continued, "And another point on control. I've been able to work with a team of professionals who, as part of a total cancer treatment plan, teach patients about death. The senior oncologist feels that there is strong evidence that many people die as they have lived."

"What does he mean?" asked the man.

"It's back again to this issue of fearing a low quality of death. He observes that patients who live a resentful life many times experience a 'resentful' death, full of prolonged suffering. And likewise, many patients who live a life of anger may experience an 'angry' death. But also, those who live a life of love, joy, and peace nearly always reflect this in their death.

"Again, the lesson here is to love. We can choose to love now, to be joyful now and to make peace of mind real now. In short, we can choose to 'live fully as long as we live' by showing love to ourselves and to those around us. The result in terms of quality of death is almost always a reflection of that way of life. Very little time is spent actually dying; the time is spent living and loving as long as we are alive."

"I like that," said the man as he took a moment to ponder the point.

The man seemed touched by the hope in the Cancer Conqueror's message. There was a comfort in understanding that he could control the quality of death by the quality of his life. And the idea of extending the reach

Choose
To Live
Fully
As Long
As We
Live!

of one's life through the memories of others—by loving others—was also reassuring.

But what about himself after death? Was he just a memory? That seemed less than fully satisfying.

"What about life after death?" asked the man. "Do you think there is more to come after this life?"

Without hesitation the Cancer Conqueror answered, "To me the evidence is overwhelming. I believe that you and I are much more than a body. I certainly do not pretend to know everything about this issue. Yet I believe very strongly that death is the exit from this life and the entrance to the next plane of existence. To me, death doesn't have to be approached with fear. I think we can approach it with a healthy curiosity of what will be next. It can be viewed as a new adventure. Can you grasp that possibility?"

The man was deep in thought. Finally he looked at the Cancer Conqueror and almost in a whisper asked, "There's comfort in those beliefs, isn't there?"

The Cancer Conqueror nodded, "For me there is. There's real comfort and real hope. I believe there is much that awaits me after life here on earth. But my concept of life, not death, is what makes the difference. This compels me to love now. The result is inner harmony and personal peace about whatever may be on the next plane."

The man stopped again. He was considering some of the implications of what the Cancer Conqueror was saying. "The next plane. Inner harmony. Personal peace. This almost has a mystical quality to it. Does the cancering journey become some sort of religious experience?"

"Some people would not be comfortable with the words *religious* or *mystical*. I prefer to use the term *spiritual* when we discuss this. And yes," said the Cancer Conqueror, "in my experience, cancering becomes very much a spiritual journey."

"Then please help me understand this part," said the man.

"Just consider the context," said the Cancer Conqueror. "We live in two worlds, the material and the spiritual. Most of our education, our efforts, even our awareness are centered in the material. But consider the cancer journey. While there is certainly a material, physical element, we move beyond that. We talk about beliefs—beliefs that are positive, that serve our health well. Then we move on to resolve, managing the emotional conflict that can depress our mind and our body's immune system. And then we make a choice, a conscious decision to LIVE. Those are all issues of the human spirit. The context becomes spiritual."

"John made that clear," said the man. "I understand the principles. But I sense I am missing a dimension. I sense this all leads somewhere."

"Excellent," said the Cancer Conqueror. "It certainly does lead somewhere. As you begin to choose the spiritual life, you'll also begin to recognize the breadth and depth of that choice. It pervades your entire life experience."

"That's good," said the man, "'. . . pervades your entire life experience.' I feel that's what is happening to me right now. I sense that I am beginning to open to a whole new life. What is actually going on here?"

The Cancer Conqueror deliberated a moment. Was the man ready for a more in-depth look at the spiritual road? Would he be able to grasp the dimensions of this choice? And could the Cancer Conqueror explain it in a way that would not alienate him? It was a tender moment. The Cancer Conqueror inched ahead.

"I can best explain this by starting once again with beliefs. This time the beliefs are not about the illness. They are about life.

"There are certain core convictions, foundational beliefs that profoundly affect our life experience in virtually every aspect. They do much to determine the quality of life on all levels. These beliefs—these core mental choices—affect us far beyond just our bodies, far beyond cancer."

"Okay," said the man, "what are they?"

"Perhaps the most fundamental belief has to do with the essence of the world in which we live. For centuries, the great thinkers have debated—what is the nature of the universe? Did biological accident or Divine direction create our experience? In short, the first core belief asks the question, 'Is there a God?'

"I encourage you to choose a healthy conviction here. I encourage you to believe that there is a God who knows us and loves us. And God loves us even though God knows us!"

"That's a healthy choice?" asked the man.

"Very healthy," said the Cancer Conqueror. "There are significant assumptions in that statement. First, there is the choice that God really does exist and that God lies behind our existence."

"Well, sometimes I'm not so sure," said the man.

The Cancer Conqueror smiled, "I can't offer you hard, scientific, rigorously researched and documented proof that there is a God. I can't take you down the street to a church and say, 'See, look at God.' On this point, trust in your beliefs is the determining factor."

"I don't know," said the man. "This is more than I am comfortable with."

The Cancer Conqueror touched the man's arm. "Look, the last thing I want to do is make you uncomfortable. But *I* am not the one who is making you uncomfortable. *You* are making you uncomfortable."

"Okay," said the man. "But the fact remains, I just don't know that much about God."

There Is
A God
Who Knows Us
And
Loves Us.

And
God Loves Us
Even Though God
Knows Us.

"You do know that there is something outside your-self, don't you?" asked the Cancer Conqueror. "After all, you didn't make this world. And I didn't create the universe. Certainly there must be some kind of Power outside of you and me. A Greater Power is behind our existence."

"Well, from that standpoint, there must be something," said the man.

"But does that mean 'God?'"

"Perhaps you're letting the word *God* get in your way. To some people the word *God* is full of negative connotations, especially that of judgmentalism.

"In all the languages of the world, people use different names for the Deity. The most widely used in the English language is *God*. For the moment, try to drop some of your previously learned concepts about God. Would you be able to explore the spiritual path openly just for a few minutes?"

"Okay," said the man. "I can do that."

"Good," said the Cancer Conqueror. "For the moment, just accept that there is 'something' that is a Higher Power. We call that power God. Let's look again at the core belief. There is a God who knows us and loves us, and God loves us even though God knows us.

"So there is a primary conclusion, an affirmation, a conviction that acknowledges a Power behind our existence. There is a God of the world."

The Cancer Conqueror continued, "The second part of our core belief states that there is a God 'who knows us.' The implications of this statement are significant. Not only are we saying that there is a God, but we are also believing that this God is aware of you and me as individuals. You are known to God personally, by name, by thought, by spirit, by all the ways that God can identify and recognize us. This is no abstract power—this is a personal one-on-one relationship with the Central Power behind everything that exists."

The man was thoughtful. Even though he didn't speak, the Cancer Conqueror could sense his attentiveness.

"Now take our core belief another step. The belief goes on to say '. . . and God loves us!' This thought is a revolution. Not only is there a God who knows us personally, but that same God *loves* us. The very Power that created everything that exists knows and loves us! Wow!"

The man smiled at the Cancer Conqueror's enthusiasm. But perhaps this was something to be enthusiastic about. It was certainly different. The man had always thought of God as some sort of mean judge.

The Cancer Conqueror continued, "Let's finish our look at the core belief. It ends by stating, '. . . and God loves us even though God knows us.' This means that even when we don't perform to our potential, we are still loved. In the eyes of the Creator of All, we are not what we do or don't do. We receive God's love simply because we are God's creation. God chooses to love us as we are!"

The man said, "But I don't see how this influences my cancer journey."

"All this acknowledges the fact that God is for us! God wants our total wellness. Our job is to get in tune with the messages cancer is sending us, make the required changes, and accept God's love and direction for our lives!"

The man snapped, "How can that be? If God is for us, why did God give us cancer?"

The Cancer Conqueror paused and smiled that serene smile. He understood how critical his next words would be. "I don't believe God did give us cancer," he said. "My belief is that this illness is not God's will, but is really the result of our deviation from God's will.

"In fact, I now believe that those things which bring

sorrow, distress, or even calamity and suffering are ultimately present in the world not as God's will, but as a
result of our misunderstanding or our deviation from
God's will."

"Well maybe," said the man, "but it seems to me that
God at least allowed the cancer."

"Perhaps," said the Cancer Conqueror. "But even that
is not the perspective you'll need to conquer cancer. The
key is to understand the message. It is really an opportunity for us to change. I've even thought of cancer as a
gift, a valuable opportunity to reshape my life. And
when I began to understand the depth of this, my whole
thinking about God and my life changed."

There was silence. The two men looked squarely into
each others' eyes. The man sat with clenched jaw, pondering the implications of what was being said. The Cancer Conqueror sent up a silent prayer, "Speak through me
now, Lord," and then continued.

"Understanding the meaning and message in cancer
brings us face to face with our second core belief. It has
to do with the nature of our life experiences. There are
many ways to say this. But the one which communicates
best to me says, 'Life is a loving teacher.'"

"If God loves us," continued the Cancer Conqueror,
"God will want the best for us. God will lovingly guide
and direct our paths. Thus through our life experiences—
both pleasant and unpleasant—lessons are going to be
taught."

"I have trouble believing that a God who is lovingly
trying to teach us would be so cruel as to cause or even
allow cancer. That's just not loving."

"Now think," continued the Cancer Conqueror firmly,
"of the consistency with the earlier belief that cancer is a
process and a message to change. Some lessons that God
lovingly gives, or even allows, are pleasant. Other lessons

Life

Is

A

Loving

Teacher.

are anything but pleasant. Yet both teach, guide, and direct our lives. Perhaps there are times when we get so off the track that the only way God can get our attention is through an event that is nearly catastrophic."

"This sounds like the vindictive, judge-type God that I was taught about as a child," said the man.

"Not so," countered the Cancer Conqueror. "God is not some unreasonable and impulsive sovereign. This is a loving God who has created a universe that runs by natural laws. This loving God doesn't give out punishment on a whim."

"But God is omnipotent," said the man. "God can do anything God wants to do."

"Certainly," said the Cancer Conqueror, "but also recognize that God has put in place the natural laws that run the world. And God seldom breaks those laws. They are the natural order of this world.

"It is healthy to believe that even cancer is a message for us to become more aligned with those natural laws. That is what life is trying to teach us—to become more aligned with God's will."

"That's hard for me to accept," said the man.

"Think of it this way, then," said the Cancer Conqueror. "Illness and health send us messages, negative and positive. Both messages tell us how we are doing. Health, happiness, peace, joy, and love are all intended as messages that we are doing well. Illness, pain—both physical and psychological—depression, fear, and despair are all negative messages that are intended to bring us back on course. They are all loving teachers."

The man shook his finger at the Cancer Conqueror. "But your logic is all wrong. The true nature of people is not good, it is evil. I can remember the exact words I was taught, '. . . man is by nature sinful and unclean.' It doesn't make sense to have a loving God who is a loving teacher if people are inherently bad. These lessons you talk about would never get through. You need to punish evil."

The Cancer Conqueror was dismayed. These were all learned beliefs and behavior—real roadblocks that had been constructed in the man's spiritual path. But they explained the man's behavior.

"No, no, no!" said the Cancer Conqueror. "Emphatically no! I don't like to confront you, but this is an important point. There is a better way. There are better beliefs! In fact, this is core belief number three—God created people in innocence and goodness.

"I went through this struggle," said the Cancer Conqueror. "I was taught that original sin had left me totally helpless, that some people are predestined to live in eternal despair and that my behavior could be controlled only with a heavy dose of fear and guilt. I was frightened by a God who I thought was out to get me.

"These beliefs are not true. They confuse what a person does with the way God originally created people. In point of fact, virtually all religions acknowledge that people were created in innocence and goodness. The concept of 'evil' we hear so many people emphasize came later.

"When the emphasis is on 'evil,' guilt almost always is the end result. This is sad and destructive. These teachings simply do not go deep enough. And worse, they inflict untold scars on people. It is my personal belief that many illnesses, including cancer, may be caused or prolonged because people condemn themselves and others with this guilt."

"I'm not sure what you're saying," said the man. "How does this apply to my getting well?"

The Cancer Conqueror continued, "Simply stated, if you believe either consciously or subconsciously that God created people as inherently evil, you will consider

God

Created

People

In

Innocence

And

Goodness.

yourself unworthy. And unworthiness certainly isn't a perspective of wellness."

"Well then," said the man, "what is that wellness perspective?"

"Let me encourage you to hold firmly to the conviction that people, at the very core of their being, have unlimited potential for kindness, goodness, and gentleness—particularly as they relate to God. Believe in people's ability to love. Perhaps the message behind cancer is that God can change us! Perhaps the real message of cancer is threefold: love God, love others, love ourselves."

"But there is so much evil out in the world. How can we say that people have the capacity for unlimited kindness, goodness, gentleness, and love? I think this is very much at odds with actual experience," said the man.

The Cancer Conqueror smiled. "Remember the central lesson of LIVE—nonjudgmental, unconditional love?"

"Yes I do," said the man. "It was a huge leap in personal growth for me. But how does it apply here?"

"Let's review," said the Cancer Conqueror. "First we looked within to realize that we do not have some terrible central flaw in our being that makes us hopeless. Next we looked without to realize that others were just the same and that we could learn to accept them as fellow human beings even though we may not approve of their behavior. And finally we saw our role—to be loving and forgiving without expecting to get something in return."

"Yes I know," said the man. "That liberated me. But I still don't see your point."

The Cancer Conqueror looked unwaveringly into the man's eyes. This would be a critical point for the man to grasp. He shot up another prayer for guidance.

"Just as you have been liberated by extending nonjudgmental, unconditional love to yourself and to others, know that a loving God is extending even more and greater love to you."

The Cancer Conqueror paused for several seconds before he spoke again. "And even though our behavior may not always match our potential, even though our potential for kindness, goodness, and gentleness is not fully realized, we can receive God's love because God loves us for who we are, not for what we do!"

Another long pause. "Because of God's great love, we are still acceptable even though we may be imperfect." He repeated, "We are imperfect but acceptable."

The Cancer Conqueror just stopped and fixed his gaze directly on the man's eyes. The long silence was finally broken by the whisper of the man himself.

"Imperfect but acceptable."

The Cancer Conqueror didn't say a word. He just nodded his head in agreement. Tears welled up in the man's eyes. You could sense a transformation underway.

The man sunk back in his chair. "Nobody ever explained it like this before," he said ever so quietly. "A loving, personal God, the Creator of all there is, life as a loving teacher, and people who are not rejected because of their imperfections.

"I'm not perfect, but I am acceptable and I am loved," he continued in a hushed voice. "I can't tell you what this means to me." He paused again. "This is the first time in my life that I have received and experienced and appreciated nonjudgmental, unconditional love."

The man stopped speaking. It was an emotional moment of silence.

Finally the Cancer Conqueror spoke. "This is a love that heals. This love is the gateway to that peace we are accepting. This love ultimately conquers cancer. And the bonus is that this love often cures it, too."

More silence. The man was meditating. At last he

We Are

Imperfect —

But

Acceptable!

asked, "There are no guarantees on this path, are there?"

"If you're looking for a sure cure on the purely physical level, nobody can offer you one with integrity. But on the spiritual level, the answer is right before you. You are known. You are loved. You are acceptable. Yes. It's guaranteed."

The two sat quietly. The man felt a sense of peacefulness that was completely new to him.

"I want to know more about the love of God," said the man. "Where do I turn? Do I go back to church? Do I take up religion? Do I pray day and night? What do I do next?"

The Cancer Conqueror smiled. "You may personally feel you need to do one or even all these things. That will be your decision. But start with the inner journey. Start with aligning yourself with God's love. Practice God's unconditional love without ceasing."

"And then what?" asked the man. "What did you do?"

"When I became aware that God is my Source," said the Cancer Conqueror, "I turned to the God of the Scriptures. Here I discovered a special power that could be found nowhere else."

"This," said the man, "is the very point I have so much trouble with. Can I really believe? Can I really trust this God?"

"Yes, you can," said the Cancer Conqueror. "You can trust God completely. But, don't expect God to do it all for you.

"I want you to trust three physicians. *Trust the body physicians*, your medical team. Trust their competence and their integrity to do all they can for you on a physical basis. *Trust your inner physician*, the inherent ability you possess to generate emotional harmony and physical healing. And *trust the spiritual physician*, the God who loves you and gives you peace."

"Why not just pray for God to perform a miracle?" asked the man.

"God could," said the Cancer Conqueror. "We certainly want to allow for that. And God sometimes does that. But the natural laws that God governs by are seldom broken. Law-of-nature-defying miracles are certainly the exception. But law-of-nature-consistent miracles are happening everyday. They can happen to you.

"And God is not lessened because of that. Believing in our own healing potential only goes to acknowledge our true spiritual nature."

Both men were quiet as they let these insights saturate their spirits. There was power for living here. Finally the man said, "You know, I have a sense of calm, of real peace—right now. I've never experienced this before. This is a new me."

The Cancer Conqueror smiled. This was the place where he had hoped to bring the man.

"Peace is the goal," the Cancer Conqueror continued softly. "Knowing God's peace—even if we have cancer—that's what it really means to conquer the illness.

"Our goal is peace—with self, with others, with God. And that goal is achieved by implementing the very things you have studied—Believe, Resolve, and Live!

"When the goal of peace is achieved, it may be temporary. In fact, try not to relate peace to time at all. It may be difficult to achieve that peace for more than a few minutes. If so, don't be discouraged. It is the journey, not just the destination, that is the aim."

"I think I've heard that principle elsewhere," said the man. "Is that why everyone kept referring to the 'cancer journey?'"

"It is," said the Cancer Conqueror. "It is a journey in search of God's peace. And the sooner you make it a LIVE

Our Goal Is Peace —

With Self,
With Others,
With God.

journey, the sooner you will benefit from life's lessons—
and experience your own peace."

The Cancer Conqueror continued, "Now consider this.
If cancer is a message to change, what is it that you are
being called to be and to do? Put the emphasis here
on *called*."

"What do you mean?" asked the man.

"Just this. Cancer is telling you to change. It's a call
toward a new goal and a new way. You are called to be
someone. You are called to do something. Pursue that
goal. Within it will be your reason for living.

"Don't be driven," continued the Cancer Conqueror.
"Be called. Take time to listen and respond to the call."

"That call," asked the man, "is it centered in loving and
helping others?"

"You know it is!" said the Cancer Conqueror. "Plus
responding to God's directions for your life. Your call
will take the form of love toward self, love toward others,
and love toward God. And you'll know you are succeed-
ing when what you think, what you say, and what you do
are consistent with God's directions."

Again the two men sat in silence. There was peace in
this silence. The Cancer Conqueror prayed. The man was
listening to that call from within.

Finally the Cancer Conqueror spoke. "The achieving is
in the doing. Go and do."

There was another silence. Finally the two men stood
and embraced. And then the man left silently. God's
peace was with him.

SECTION 7

The Cancer Conqueror Benefits

*A*s the weeks passed, the man put to use what he had learned. And guess what happened?

He became a Cancer Conqueror!

It happened not just because the man talked like a Cancer Conqueror, but because he had learned a better way to LIVE!

And as the weeks built into months, he realized that it was not simply that he had learned new skills and knowledge, but that he *did* what he had learned.

This *was* a better life. Cancer really *was* a signal to change. New freedom was his! Love, joy, and peace were real to him!

At the end of the first year, the man looked back to the day when he had first met the Cancer Conqueror. Since that time, he had changed so much. His beliefs about cancer were radically different. And he had begun to resolve some fundamental problems he hadn't even recognized prior to the cancer. And LIVE had given him freedom he had barely imagined.

The man was thrilled to understand for the first time in his life that he really was the one in control. But it was a control unlike the control that most people sought.

For certainly the man was not the Ultimate Power. Nor was he immune to all the problems life had to offer! But rather the man had developed a new power over himself, a power within, which allowed him to choose how to react to the events of life. He had begun to align himself with God's will. This is where the power and control came from. This was living! This was Conquering Cancer!

The man began sharing his own journey with newly-diagnosed patients. It was most encouraging to see people change their beliefs, resolve their difficulties, and then choose to LIVE!

The man made himself more and more available for these times of sharing. Cancer had taught him some valuable lessons. He was becoming a student of life. And at the same time, he was becoming a teacher of living.

He enjoyed helping others learn to help themselves.

Perhaps what he enjoyed most, though, was the mastery over his own life. Every day, in every way, he was learning to LIVE!

He felt capable of dealing with today in a way that helped others as he helped himself and the world in which he lived.

The phone rang.

A young woman introduced herself. She explained that she had just been diagnosed with cancer. "I have been told that I have a journey ahead of me. I know I have a lot to learn. I would like to learn from the best. May I come talk to you?"

The man smiled that serene smile he had seen so many times before. Now he realized the smile was a sign that all was well—*very* well!

It felt good to be in this position. He *had* learned a great deal. He was one of the most significant success stories because he had come from despair to hope. Now he knew inner peace—God's peace. It was a simple journey. But it had not been easy.

"Of course you can come talk with me," he answered.

As soon as the young woman arrived, he began the conversation. "I'm happy to share my experiences with you. In doing so, I have just one request."

"What is that?" she asked.

"That you share this hope with others!"

Bible Study Guide

Cancer &
the Greatest
Healing Promises
from the Bible

Week 1

Do Not Fear

Getting Started

Begin with prayer.

And Samuel said to the people, "Do not be afraid; you have done all this evil, yet do not turn aside from following the Lord, but serve the Lord with all your heart; and do not turn aside after useless things that cannot profit or save, for they are useless. For the Lord will not cast away his people, for his great name's sake, because it has pleased the Lord to make you a people for himself. Moreover as for me, far be it from me that I should sin against the Lord by ceasing to pray for you; and I will instruct you in the good and the right way. Only fear the Lord, and serve him faithfully with all your heart; for consider what great things he has done for you.
       I Samuel 12:20-24 (NRSV)

The people of Israel had a choice. Now that God had legitimized the nation by permitting and finding a king for them, they as a community could choose one of two responses — they could resolve to be obedient to God's covenant still open to them or they could rebel against God and bring exile and the loss of the very monarchy which they believed would bring them victory.

There are two good reasons for hope revealed in this passage. First, Israel finally had a king, a leader, as well as prophets, to intercede for the people and clearly and unambiguously reveal God's will to them. Second, however fallible and forgetful Israel might be, God had chosen them for God's own purposes and therefore God would never demean his own reputation by abandoning them.

The message of this passage to the people of Israel was this — the people need not fear. For despite their past failings and present weakness, the future offered much hope and promise for them. They were revealed as God's own and therefore God would never abandon them. The message is the same for us today. We are God's own people too. And like the ancient people of Israel, we have choices every day in our lives, choices that can lead us to accept God and God's comfort and loving kindness or choices that reject God and the help, support, strength and victory God reaches out to give.

- *What is your choice today?*
- *Why is it often difficult to choose to be positive?*
- *Where do we see evidence that God is reaching out to help us every day?*
- *How have you experienced God's grace this day?*

Understanding What We Believe

Personal Responsibility: Gaining a Sense of Control

The degree to which a patient takes personal responsibility for his or her own actions and feelings in response to a cancer diagnosis is a crucially important determinant of the course of an illness. Awareness and choice are the twin towering pillars that support personal responsibility.

We increase awareness through our personal research and education, becoming an eager student, ready to learn everything we can about our diagnosis and range of treatment options. From this knowledge base, we then exercise our choices, giving fully-informed consent to treatments and thus make intentional choices in our physical, emotional and spiritual lifestyles.

In your own cancer journey, the power of personal responsibility is stupendous; its implications are massive. Personal responsibility is fundamental. Believe you have a role.

Recognize the potential negative consequences; if we don't give mindful attention to our diagnosis, treatment, diet, exercise, emotional outlook, and spiritual choices, we will surely not respond to cancer with optimum capacity. Ignore our personal responsibility and we fail to implement a comprehensive recovery program.

The good news is that the personal responsibility coin has two sides. Just as less-than-mindful attention will contribute to a less-than-optimal response, a fully-mindful response holds the promise of direct wellness benefits. We have the power to become aware of and make changes in our beliefs and behavior. It is as simple, and as complex, as changing our thinking.

Fear or hope? Belief or unbelief? When we believe we have a role and assume personal responsibility for our choices, we have the ability to change our every experience of cancer. Having experienced both sides of this coin, I have no doubt of personal responsibility's significant power.

After my cancerous left lung was removed, I quickly reverted to my previous behaviors. My diet consisted of too much high-fat, high-carbohydrate fast food. My exercise program was sporadic at best. I lived an adrenalin-charged, workaholic life. I demonstrated an overly critical and disagreeable spirit. I thought, "The doctor has fixed things. Now I can get back to life as usual."

I believe those unwise personal choices greatly contributed to my return to the hospital a short four months later. It was then discovered that the cancer was throughout my lymph system. The surgeon said, "Greg, the tiger is out of the cage. Your cancer has come roaring back. I would give you about thirty days to live."

There's nothing like bad news to either paralyze or energize. The 30-day prognosis focused my attention and energy. I felt I had two ways to turn. One was to give in to the despair and prepare to die. The other, even though it held no promise of success, was to participate fully in an effort to get well again. What did I really believe? I chose the latter. Today, I have come to realize the vitally important role each patient plays in his or her recovery. Central to success is assuming personal responsibility for proper diet and appropriate exercise. Stress management has a key supportive role and deserves to be understood and implemented by the serious wellness student. So do our beliefs and attitudes, the resolution of emotional conflict and hostility, plus capturing a sense of joy. And the benefits of adopting a more spiritual focus on life may be the most important recovery tool of all.

Fear or hope? Belief or unbelief? These are choices only patients can make. Nobody can get well for us. Others can help, of course. But in the final analysis, we must walk the wellness path for ourselves. We stand personally accountable for this journey. Choose.

Discussion:
Examine your current level of personal responsibility

Consider each statement. Discuss your level of agreement.

1. I am in charge of my experience of cancer.
   Discussion starters: What does "being in charge" actually mean to me? What is within my sphere of influence? Is "control" really possible, or even preferable, for me?

2. Getting well again is not just a matter of genetics and medical treatment.
   Discussion-starter: What must I personally contribute to the process beyond selecting a treatment program?

3. My personal efforts do make a difference in my recovery.
   Discussion-starter: When I think of myself as making a difference, what do I picture myself doing?

4. I have the ability to discriminate between what is controllable and what is uncontrollable in the cancer journey.
   Discussion-starters: How can I most effectively control my fears? How can I create a calm and quiet healing environment?

5. My mind and spirit have a central role in my recovery.
   Discussion-starters: Is my state of mind and spirit most often positive or negative? How do I typically demonstrate belief? Unbelief? What can I do to nurture a more positive mental and spiritual outlook?

6. Registering my emotions using "I feel . . . " instead
    of "You make me feel . . ." brings me empowerment.
    Discussion starters: Do I fully understand the
    statement: "Cancer doesn't make me fearful (angry/
    guilty), I make me fearful (angry/guilty)?" How do
    I make myself fearful (angry/guilty)? Can I truly
    master my fear (anger/guilt)? How?

7. When I have moments of feeling helpless,
    victimized, and depressed, I have ready resources
    that empower me.
    Discussion starter: Share the people, places, and
    things you can turn to truly lift mind and spirit
    — without fail?

8. I possess considerable power to create the life and
    well-being I desire.
    Thought starter: When I think of myself as well,
    what is the image I carry in my mind?

For the advanced wellness student:

When people give more power to unbelief than belief, it can
often be seen in their language. A person who says, "That
doctor makes me so mad," is shifting responsibility for his
anger onto his doctor. A breast cancer patient who says,
"I prefer to have my surgery during the second half of my
menstrual cycle," is taking responsibility for her own needs
in a more direct way.*

(*Mounting evidence exists that premenopausal women
have fewer recurrences when breast cancer surgery is per-

formed in the luteal phase, days 14-30, of the menstrual cycle. Ask your physician.)

Accusatory "you" statements can be a sign that patients and family members are blaming. Many times this happens because the person does not take responsibility, or feel permitted, to say, "I don't like what is happening in my life at this time." Instead, the words come out as, "You (or the doctor, or the nurse, or the receptionist, or God) are unfair (or unkind, or not caring, or unloving) and make me upset."

Examine your own behavior. "You" statements indicate that the speaker holds someone else responsible for his happiness and well-being. The speaker thus gives up considerable personal control. He depends on other people to be aware of his needs and fulfill them. Someone else is given the duty of making his personal choices. If things don't work out satisfactorily, someone else gets the blame.

Cancer patients who choose the journey to wellness tend to make "I" statements that express their own needs, feelings, likes, and dislikes. This does not mean the patient is without support or "goes it alone." Instead, there is a clear understanding among the patient, the health care team, and the primary support team, that each individual is responsible for determining how he or she will respond to cancer in his or her own life.

Become aware of your own level of personal responsibility. Analyze your responses to the following queries. Are they true or false? Why might you be reacting that way? List several ways you might change.

1. *Cancer doesn't make me fearful, I make myself fearful.*
2. *The doctor doesn't make me angry, I make myself angry.*
3. *My husband (wife/partner/child/friend) doesn't make me feel guilty, I make myself feel guilty.*
4. *God doesn't make me feel abandoned, I make myself feel abandoned.*

What kinds of feelings about belief, unbelief and personal responsibility do these queries evoke? Does this task of personal responsibility seem to be too much for you? In what ways and areas?

Blame is one of the surest ways to stay mired in a problem and "stuck" in unbelief. When we blame another person, or God, we give away our power. The moment we become aware and begin to understand this dynamic, we rise above the issue and take responsibility for our responses.

Don't blame the past; it cannot be changed. Don't blame the fear of an unknown future; we shape our future by our current state of mind and spirit. Don't blame doctors or hospitals or health care insurers or parents or spouses or God.

Most important, don't blame or demand perfection from yourself. If you do, you will be miserable every waking moment. Don't blame. Instead, channel that energy into creating a place in your mind and spirit where you are well. Then live from that place.

Encourage further sharing among your group.

Close with prayer.

Week 2

Belief or Unbelief

Getting Started

Begin with prayer.

Someone from the crowd answered him, "Teacher, I brought you my son; he has a spirit that makes him unable to speak; and whenever it seizes him, it dashes him down; and he foams and grinds his teeth and becomes rigid; and I asked your disciples to cast it out, but they could not do so." He answered them, "You faithless generation, how much longer must I be among you? How much longer must I put up with you? Bring him to me." And they brought the boy to him. When the spirit saw him, immediately it convulsed the boy, and he fell on the ground and rolled about, foaming at the mouth. Jesus asked the father, "How long has this been happening to him" And he said, "From childhood. It has often cast him into the fire and into the water, to destroy him; but if you are able to do anything, have pity on us and help us." Jesus said to him, "If you are able!" All things can be done for the one who believes." Immediately the father of the child cried out, "I believe; help my unbelief!"
     Mark 9:17-24 (NRSV)

A father is desperate to have his son cured of epilepsy, so he brings the child to Jesus' disciples, hoping they can help. But the disciples are unable to deal with the boy's condition. Their inability gives members of the religious establishment, who are looking for reasons to attack them, cause to belittle and criticize Jesus and his disciples.

. Jesus has just literally come down from a glorious moun-
taintop experience — the Transfiguration — where he, witnessed by his disciples Peter, James and John, was revealed
to be God's true Son, the one legitimate successor to the
prophet Elijah and Moses, the heir and embodiment of God's
power and might. From this awe-inspiring moment, Jesus
comes down into the harsh realities of the everyday world,
where people suffer, struggle and fear. In doing so he proves
himself to be one who is not only concerned with cosmic
issues of eternal glory, but also issues of basic human dilemma. Jesus came to save the entire world. But he proves
here that he came to help us as individuals, too.

Jesus comes down from the mountain of transfiguration
to find his own disciples beaten down, baffled, helpless and
ineffective. He finds a father and son desperate for healing
and relief. In the midst of the despair and anxiety of the
situation around him, Jesus chooses to act and deal with
the circumstance at hand. Even though the disciples and
the boy's father all express a paradoxical unbelieving faith,
Jesus shows compassion on them and heals the child of his
distress. Even though the father expresses doubt and uncertainty, he is willing to try anything and cries out for help.
His imperfect faith still produces healing, because he cares
deeply about his son and reaches out in desperation on his
son's behalf. Even though the disciples show ineffectiveness
and impotence, their mentor and leader, Jesus, proves they
are following the right one.

This passage addresses any disciple or group frustrated by
impotence — spiritual, emotional, intellectual, physical. It
reminds us that Jesus — God in the flesh — has authority
over distressing and demonic forces and can handle any problem we bring. And it encourages us to trust more in God,
because God — the source of help and wholeness — does
work in and through us to heal ourselves and one another.

A great promise is offered — God provides us with the relief and new life we need. A great truth is revealed — our failures are often related to our unbelief in the possibilities that God can fulfill. But with a father's *openness to the possibilities, in spite of his doubts,* God is allowed to step in. To approach anything in the spirit of hopelessness is to make things hopeless. To approach life in the spirit of faith is to make new life possible. We do not allow miracles to manifest themselves because we are too often cursed with a sense of the impossible. The world and its ways may disappoint us, but God never does.

- *In what ways have you lacked belief in God's power to help?*
- *In what ways have others had faith on your behalf and you have been helped by their faith?*
- *How do our attitudes and beliefs negatively or positively affect our well-being?*
- *How can you gain more faith?*

Understanding What We Believe

Beliefs:
Recovering a Sense of the Possible

"Change your mind, change your health." That may be truer than we ever dared believe. Beliefs create actions. Actions create results. Results confirm beliefs. This is how self-fulfilling prophecies become reality.

Throughout the annals of cancer there are legions of people who, despite all odds, succeeded in achieving wellness. They found strength to carry them over, under, around, and through seemingly insurmountable obstacles. I believe the same is possible for you.

One of the chief barriers to attaining and accepting healing is the limits imposed by our beliefs. We have limited notions of what we can accomplish. Many times we believe healing is not possible, that our personal case is fundamentally different, or that while others may be able to effect healing, we lack the inner resources or the moral goodness to attain wellness.

What follows are some suggestions for your thoughtful consideration. These are offered lovingly; I'm not demanding answers to any one of these queries. I simply invite exploration of the set of beliefs which you bring to the cancer recovery process.

Knowing that we all live somewhere between belief and disbelief, rate yourself openly and honestly. There are no right or wrong answers. Unless you choose to share, you are the only one who will see your responses. Thousands of fellow cancer survivors have found it highly empowering to explore the implications of the beliefs they hold. I predict you will benefit too.

1. Cancer is more than a physical illness.
    *Discussion starters: Do I believe that cancer is
    something more than cellular biology? What
    cultural and scientific beliefs does this challenge?*

2. Cancer is not synonymous with my death.
    *Discussion starters: Is a belief like this empowering
    or actually self-deception? What might result,
    positively or negatively, if I whole-heartedly
    embrace this belief? What benefits might result if
    I whole-heartedly embrace this belief? What if
    I reject it?*

3. My cancer cells are weak and confused.
    *Discussion starters: What mental picture of cancer
    cells do I carry? What image might serve me best?*

4. My treatment plan is highly effective.
    *Discussion starters: Do I understand how the actual
    therapy is intended to work? Does it seem
    scientifically plausible? Is it consistent with known
    principles? What is my confidence level in the
    practitioner and the allied health care providers? Is
    the treatment delivered in an environment that is
    physically safe and emotionally nurturing?*

5. The side effects of my treatment are minor and can
    be largely controlled.
    *Discussion starter: What specifically do I fear most
    about potential side effects?*

6. My immune system has the potential to effectively
    control malignant cells.
    *Discussion starter: What could I do to further
    enhance my immune function?*

7. I am in charge of my total treatment plan.
    *Discussion starters: What elements, beyond
    medicine, can I add to enhance my total treatment
    plan? How can I remain in charge of this program?*

8. I am "cancering," experiencing a process, as opposed
    to having cancer, trapped in a negative condition.
    *Discussion starters: How is this understanding
    different from the strictly biological definition of
    cancer? How does this understanding empower me?*

9. Emotional, psychological, and spiritual health is a choice.
   Discussion starter: What can I do to choose wellness during times of doubt and fear?

10. Cancer is a message for me to change.
    Discussion starter: Areas for change that might produce immediate benefits in my well-being include:

Diet _____

Exercise _____

Medical treatment _____

Emotional outlook _____

Relationships _____

Beliefs _____

Attitudes _____

Career _____

Purpose in life _____

Spiritual life _____

Other _____

For the advanced wellness student

With a cancer diagnosis, feelings of hope and despair are in a constant tug-of-war. One day we may tune in the message of healing but the next day discount it as misguided or impossible. Wellness can be elusive. As soon as the situation looks desperate, we rule out what is possible before allowing the potential to unfold.

It amazes me how many cancer patients do not believe they can get well. Think of a bell-shaped curve; I have observed that at one end, 10-15 percent of patients actually welcome cancer and consider it an honorable way to die. In the middle of the curve, 70-80 percent of patients seem to just go along, dutifully fulfilling their passive role assigned by the doctor. At the far end of the curve is another 10-15 percent. These are the cancer conquerors. The most profound difference . . . is the set of underlying beliefs this group brings to the process.
        -Greg Anderson,
        PBS Television Special
        "Creating Incredible Wellness"

Beliefs, and the resulting attitudes and expectations, constantly contribute to actual experience in all areas of life. This includes the experience of cancer. This much is clear: beliefs can be chosen. But we seldom consciously choose them. Perhaps beliefs have simply been accepted by us for many years, like the conventional wisdom surrounding cancer. Perhaps we had beliefs imposed from parents, co-workers, or friends. We may have picked up other people's beliefs and made them our own. They may or may not be true or helpful.

Look deeply, deeper than ever before, and take a searching personal inventory that will heighten your awareness of your beliefs. Please respond in the open spirit of self-discovery:

One belief I have heard others espouse about cancer is:
My greatest fear about cancer is:
My fear of cancer stands in the way of my wellness by:

Believe it or not, we can change our beliefs. We may habitually choose the same belief over and over: "I'm going to die of breast cancer just like my mother." "Oh no, ovarian cancer is so painful and frightening." "I may fight, but the cancer means my eventual demise." The fundamental belief is, cancer means death. It may not seem as if we are choosing the belief; but we did make the original choice.

You may wish to challenge some beliefs. Share your response to these prompts:

- *Three beliefs that would immediately help me begin to heal are:*
- *One deeply-held belief I would like to change:*
- *One way to accomplish this is:*

Beliefs can also be hidden and still remain a powerful guiding force. If we are honest, we recognize there are moments when we are our own worst enemy. On the one hand, we take ourselves seriously and don't want to look like a fool pursuing some false hope of recovery. On the other hand, we don't take ourselves — or God — seriously enough. Increasing our awareness of hidden beliefs increases our ability to respond positively.

- *Ways I make myself sick:*
- *I become ill when I try to avoid:*
- *When I was sick as a child, my mother always:*

Are any of these "hidden belief factors" adversely influencing your journey to wellness? If so, how does this awareness direct you to respond?

Personal beliefs establish personal parameters. I ask you to believe in your vast God-given potential for cancer recovery.

I have seen it in my own life; I believe it is equally possible for you. Just because you now have cancer does not automatically mean you will have it a year from now. Cancer is a reversible disease. Believe it.

Are you aware of all your wellness assets? Awareness is the first step in deploying them. You and I are able to draw physically, emotionally and spiritually, on an unlimited wellness account. We tend to draw very limited amounts compared to the resources available to us. This is the hour to tap into all your substantial resources.

Today, vow to believe recovery is possible . . . for you . . . beginning now.

Encourage further sharing among your group.

Close with prayer.

Week 3

Pray & Forgive

Getting Started

Begin with prayer.

Are any among you suffering? They should pray. Are you cheerful? They should sing songs of praise. Are any among you sick? They should call for the elders of the church and have them pray over them, anointing them with oil in the name of the Lord. The prayer of faith will save the sick, and the Lord will raise them up; and anyone who has committed sins will be forgiven. Therefore confess your sins to one another, and pray for one another, so that you may be healed. The prayer of the righteous is powerful and effective.
James 5:13-16 (NRSV)

One characteristic of the early church was its focus on healing, an emphasis inherited from its Jewish roots. When a Jew was ill, a visit was made to a rabbi, where anointing with oil and prayers were offered. The early church was devotedly attentive to those who were sick and even appointed widows to care for women who were ill. For many centuries the church consistently and formally used anointing as a ministry of healing, but not as a form of medicine. The sacrament of unction was, in the early church, designed as a means leading to a cure. Its current function in the Roman Catholic Church as a preparation for death did not begin until the ninth century C.E.

This passage emphasizes the communal character of Christian life. Above all, it conveys the idea that no limits can be set to the power of prayer. To people of faith it means no less than contacting and connecting with the power of God, the channel through which the strength and grace of God are brought to bear on the troubles and problems of life. It acknowledges our need to be in communion with God and one another to overcome and find victory over the ills, pains, disappointments, fears and discouragements of life. Prayer also helps to break the barriers of silence and isolation that illness often imposes on those who are ill and their families. This passage reminds us that God *does* hear our cries when we are distressed and *is* in communion with us in all our moments of need.

- *What barriers in your life do you need to begin to break down?*
- *What prevents you from praying to God and listening for God's response?*
- *How can the community around you enable you to live more abundantly?*
- *How can communion with God enable you to live more abundantly?*

Examining What We Believe

Resolve:
Letting Go of Fear, Anger and Guilt

Most of us carry around a lot of emotional baggage. The contents are mostly variations of fear, anger and guilt. This load is unnecessary and may have even contributed to the onset of cancer. Prayer and forgiveness are required. The good news: unburdening ourselves often contributes to healing.

Emotional release opens the gateways to healing. The link between emotions and health is rapidly gaining a significant foundation of scientific proof. Dr. Yujiro Ikemi and colleagues in Kyoto, Japan conducted a retrospective study of long-term survivors from cancers usually considered terminal. Why did they live? The patients all reported the onset of the disease during a time of severe "existential crisis." The patients then used the diagnosis of cancer as an opportunity to resolve the issues that led up to the disease. Finally, the patients committed themselves to carrying out God's will in their lives.

Dr. Steven Greer at King's College Hospital in England compared a group of women treated with mastectomy for breast cancer. Survival was nearly three times greater among those who developed a fighting spirit in response to the diagnosis compared to those who felt hopeless and helpless.

Psychosocial studies of cancer patients here in the United States confirm these findings. Dr. David Spiegel at Stanford University directed a study of breast cancer patients who participated in emotionally-expressive groups. The findings: participants lived twice as long as non-participants.

At UCLA, Fawzy Fawzy, M.D., followed malignant melanoma patients who participated in emotionally-supportive groups. Participants who took part in a six-week program that taught better emotional coping skills lived twice as long as control groups who did not participate.

Your appreciation of the link between emotions and health is an important part of understanding Jesus' command to, "Rise up." The following exercises focus on increasing emotional awareness and defining optimal emotional choices. As the very word "optimal" implies, perfect emotional awareness and the ideal emotional response are eternally unattainable goals; even the very best of us fall short some of the time. Yet there remains a healthy emotional direction that holds out the very real hope of healing. These queries point you in that direction.

Consider each statement. Indicate your level of belief by briefly sharing your level of acceptance of each belief.

1. I live with a vital awareness that my emotions have a major role in determining my health. *Discussion starters: How compelling do I consider the current scientific evidence regarding the mind-body-spirit connection? If I accept this concept, what are the implications concerning my current state of health?*

2. I am aware of and can identify my emotions. *Discussion starters: Share circumstances that nearly always elicit fearful emotions from you. Share three that elicit anger. And three that produce feelings of guilt. What thoughts typically precede each of these emotional responses?*

3. I am typically able to ask, "Does this situation warrant my becoming fearful (angry/guilty)?" *Discussion starter: Share a favorite personal response, such as, "Oh well, it's only my emotions," that could counter your negative responses to emotionally-charged people and circumstances.*

4. I recognize and control emotions which are aimed at affixing blame on others or me. *Discussion starter: Identify the people or circumstances to whom you have attached blame for your emotional upsets. Write the persons' name and/or the circumstances below.*

5. I am appropriately assertive, making my needs
    known at the right time and in the right manner.
    *Discussion starters: List three things to which you
    recently should have said, "No." List three recent
    events where you were overly-assertive? What has
    been their toll on your health?*

6. I carefully listen to others — and to myself — and
    am able to discern motives and intention.
    *Discussion starters: Describe a recent circumstance
    where you listened with great care and were able
    to clearly understand the "why" behind the actions
    and events? How do you sense this was of
    emotional benefit to you?*

7. I am able to practice the healthful art of forgiveness
    and release.
    *Discussion starter: Share one circumstance, and the
    corresponding emotions, of which you need to learn
    to let go.*

8. I value myself and refuse to suffer through either
    despair or denial as I travel the cancer journey.
    *Discussion starter: Share one personal response you
    have found helpful in replacing emotions of fear,
    anger, and guilt with happiness, joy, and personal
    peace.*

9. I recognize cancer is, among other things, asking of
    me a different emotional lifestyle.
    *Discussion starters: From an emotional perspective,
    what are you gaining from this illness? Describe
    one example of how this illness is giving you
    permission to meet an emotional need for love,
    acceptance, or control. How might that need be
    better fulfilled? What changes will that require?*

10. Forgiveness does not mean condoning the
    destructive behavior of others or excusing similar
    behavior in myself.
    *Discussion starters: Are we required to "forgive
    and forget?" Is it better to "forgive and learn?"
    What does "release" mean to you.*

For the advanced wellness student

The first step in resolving emotional conflict is an inward one;
we must notice the typical emotional road maps by which we
navigate. Awareness starts the process. If you completed the
foregoing exercises, you now have a keener insight into your
emotional patterns. But there are subtler emotional lifestyle
issues that may be part of the experience of cancer. They relate
to the ways that cancer can actually benefit us.

At first glance, most people are surprised that having cancer
carries any benefits at all. It does. Cancer most often changes
the way people relate to one another. Many patients and support people develop new, usually more spiritual, perspectives
on life. And cancer is often the catalyst to filling some unmet
emotional needs. These side benefits can be positive and most
meaningful. Hundreds of patients have shared, "I know this
sounds strange, but I am actually thankful I went through the
cancer experience." For these people, life takes on a new quality.
Cancer has helped them live fuller and richer lives.

Some of these "secondary gains" have a darker side. Cancer can serve as a powerful lever to manipulate and control others. Our society sanctions it because life-threatening illness is a powerful cultural force. People who become sick are likely to receive certain automatic benefits. We tend to treat them better than people who are healthy. Certainly, when people are ill they need treatment and nourishment — physically, emotionally, and spiritually. And it is wonderful when people receive it.

But many people feel as if they must become ill or stay ill in order to receive love and attention. In effect, we reward the ill and punish or withhold rewards from the well. Much is expected from those who are healthy; expectations are lowered for those with life-threatening illness. It's a widely-accepted cultural norm.

To the extent that cancer is a means of fulfilling emotional needs, it tends to be critically important to many patients. People cling to and protect that which is important. We say, "Oh no, surely that's not me." Let's be certain. Please share in an open, non-judgmental spirit of self-discovery:

- *The relationship that has changed most from my experience with cancer is . . .*
- *This relationship has changed in the following ways . . .*
- *Other relationships, responsibilities, and expectations that have changed as a result of my cancer include . . .*

Cancer comes bearing gifts. It is important to recognize those positive secondary gains so that the patient and the entire family can incorporate the benefits into daily life. Share your response to the following prompts:

- *Cancer gave me the gift of permission to express my feelings and ask for my needs to be met in these areas . . .*
- *Cancer gave me the gift of not taking the following for granted . . .*
- *Cancer gave me the gift to stop postponing . . .*
- *Cancer gave me the gift of being able to say "no" to . . .*
- *Cancer gave me the gift of not basing my life on what other people may think of me in the areas of . . .*

Now the issue is to maintain the positive gains and without using cancer as a tool of leverage. Our emotional needs for love and compassion are legitimate. Improving the quality of life, for ourselves and others, is an appropriate priority. Personal growth is a worthy pursuit. Cancer, and the transformation it calls us to make, can be the gateway to all this and more.

Perhaps it is time to consider some future strategies on living and how to maintain the real gains of cancer. Ask yourself such questions as:

- *How can I continue to communicate more authentically than I did before I learned about my cancer diagnosis?*
- *How can I allow more autonomy for myself and permit more autonomy for my family and loved ones?*
- *What must I do to maintain the internal permissions cancer gave to me without clinging to the disease?*
- *When I think of being well again, what do I imagine will change?*
- *When I think of being well again, do I imagine I will once again fill my responsibilities with similar*

intensity and at such breakneck speed? How will it
be different?
• *When I think of being well again, will I still feel*
  subject to the same pressures at work and at home?
• *How will it be different?*
• *When I think of being well again, will I still be able to*
  say "no" when I feel like it?

Your emotional lifestyle is central to your recovery from cancer. You have the ability to choose your emotions, everyday, in every situation. In the past, we have allowed emotions to be chosen for us, accepting what came without regard for our well-being. Most times, this strategy did not serve us well. Be aware. Choose. Rise up.

Close with prayer, *anointing with oil those who wish such prayer.*

Week 4

Praying for Connection

Getting Started

Begin with prayer.

*You ask and you do not receive, because you ask wrongly.
God opposes the proud, but gives grace to the humble. Submit
yourselves therefore to God. Resist the devil, and he will flee
from you. Draw near to God, and he will draw near to you.
Humble yourselves before the Lord and he will exalt you.*
        Selected verses from James 4 (NRSV)

*Pray then in this way: "Our Father in heaven, hallowed be
your name ..."*
        Matthew 6:9 (NRSV)   The Lord's Prayer

In the fourth chapter, James writes about the values in
human society that are hostile to God and asks a basic question: is our aim in life to submit to the will of God or is our
aim to gratify our own desires for the temporary pleasures
of this world? We are challenged with the principle that if
only pleasure is the aim, then nothing but strife, hatred and
division can follow. The New Testament is very clear that
an over-desire for the pleasures of this world is always a
threatening danger to our spiritual life. The ultimate choice
in life lies between pleasing ourselves versus pleasing God.
It is impossible for God to answer prayers that center only
on ourselves. We cannot even pray in the right way until
we remove ourselves from the center of life and put God
there instead.

This passage also reminds us that when we place ourselves above others we exhibit arrogance or haughtiness. In doing so we show we don't know our own need. We cherish our independence too much. We don't recognize our own weakness and brokenness. And because we don't recognize our needs, we cannot ask, because we do not believe we need help. But once we understand our need, we can stand against evil; we can stand in the power of God. Humility opens the way *of* God and *to* God for us.

Throughout the Bible runs the conviction that only those who are humble can truly know the blessings of God. It is only when we realize and recognize our own ignorance that we can truly ask for God's guidance. Only when we recognize our own weakness in necessary things will we come to draw upon God's strength, which alone can answer our helplessness. If we regard ourselves as independent of God we are on our way to ultimate collapse and defeat.

Humility demands a complete reversal of our way of life. Humility is the admission of God's gifts to us and the acknowledgement that we have been given them to use for others. It is a total continuing surrender to God's power in our lives and the lives of those around us. Humility requires a change of attitude and a change of heart.

The Lord's Prayer is a prayer for Jesus' disciples, for those committed to Christ are best able to pray it with full meaning. When we know what we are saying as we pray, when we possess a deeper understanding of what God has done and can continue to do, we are most able to comprehend and live the words we pray.

The opening words of the prayer focus on God and on God's glory. They, too, remind us that when we place God first, above anyone or anything else, all other things fall into order. Before we address our own needs, placing God's will and wonder as the top priority of our lives is most essential.

Our prayers must never be an attempt to bend our will and wants to God. On the contrary, prayer must always be an attempt to listen to God, to comprehend God's will for us and to submit our lives to that will.

Beginning with the word "Our", the prayer reminds us that it is not "me" or "mine", but "us" and "we" who are in this world together. God is no one's exclusive possession. It involves the elimination of the self and looks beyond, to the needs of the entire community instead.

"Father" reminds us of a very close, special and loving relationship, one of creation, guidance and protection.

"Who art in heaven", calls us to recognize that there is a world beyond this one. It points us to a better place, a place of peace, of eternity, of perfection, of healing, a place where the distress and disease of this world are not the final word. It is a place that lifts us above this world and calls us to strive for goals that are different from those of the world around us.

"Hallowed be thy name" calls us to treat God's name differently and uniquely from all other names. In Hebrew, the language in which the psalms were originally written, "name" means the character, personality and nature of a person. In other words, it says, "enable us to give you the unique place which your nature and character deserve."

The Lord's Prayer calls for reverence, humility, and a deep awareness of God. It is a reminder of God's love for us, of God's justice in righting all that is wrong, and of God's holiness, of one who is beyond and different from the rest of the world and who can lift us beyond it too.

- *When have you felt disconnected from God?*
- *How do you find a connection and know that God is listening and responding to your needs?*

- *In what ways do you allow other priorities to push God out of your everyday life?*
- *How can you find more humility and achieve dependence on God's goodness and grace?*

Understanding What We Believe

Cancer Conquerors Transcend

Your soul and spirit, that immaterial and vital intelligence that animates you, is incredibly powerful. Optimal health and well-being is the by-product of your physical, mental, emotional, and spiritual factors. Yet our soul is often the most misunderstood and least-utilized of our considerable healing resources.

Soul and spirit are much more than a mere resource; they are our very essence. All us of are spiritual beings. We are a "chip off the divine block." To be spiritual implies a conscious awareness of that power that is our ultimate nature, as well as a conscious connection with a dimension of Ultimate Intelligence that is greater than us. Awareness of our connection — this is the key.

Spirituality is founded on a recognition that life is sacred and has been given to us as a gift. The fact that cancer may temporarily obscure a portion of this gift in no way diminishes its priceless value.

It is easy to lose sight of the spiritual component of life. We struggle with cancer, forgetting that pain can be an opportunity for spiritual awakening. We hope the wonders of modern medicine will restore our vitality. Yet we forget that the root definition of health is "wholeness," which includes mending the spirit.

One of the most significant redeeming opportunities of cancer is that we are given ample favorable circumstances to discover the transcendent dimension of life. "Is there really a God?" "What is my life's purpose?" "What am I on this earth to accomplish?" In two decades of personally working with over 15,000 cancer patients, I can report without equivocation that nurturing a deeper spirituality is central to healing. It is awesome and predictable; when people move beyond medical care, diet, exercise, stress management, they invariably come to the journey of the soul. It is often a turning point, for this is the terrain of healing. It is also virgin territory for most people. Cancer has brought them to the frontier of their existence. The conversations typically turn quiet and serious, as if we just crossed a threshold into the most tender and sacred aspects of life.

I have been exceedingly fortunate to be a healing guide to many people and have witnessed a wide variety of very intimate spiritual experiences. I can report that one size does not fit all. Some people have "reflex" spiritual answers: "I turned my troubles over to God and decided to live to be a hundred." Or, "I just let go and let God." For many others, the soul's journey through cancer is an introduction to humility. A powerful business executive, diagnosed with metastatic prostate cancer, shook his head and quietly said, "When I realized this situation was out of my control, the only comfort I had was a belief in the ultimate goodness of God."

The portals of healing are opened in many ways. Religious orientation is less the deciding factor than a conscious awareness of a personal reciprocal, loving connection with the Divine. Ponder thoughtfully the words: conscious, awareness, personal, reciprocal, loving, connection. I am persuaded that this type of spiritual transcendence, over time, has demonstrated power to help people heal. At the least, it is central to recovering a sense of balance, tranquility, and hope. And, as I have both experienced and observed, those conditions of the soul are very often prerequisites for a cure. Whether it is a fundamentalist's fervent belief in the power of prayer or an agnostic's deep reverence for life, I have come to understand there is nothing in medicine that equals the power of standing consciously in the awesome presence of God.

Awaken your spirit

Consider each statement. Share your reflections on your level of intensity surrounding each belief.

1. There is a power, God, who is greater than I am or any human being.
   Discussion starters: Am I comfortable calling that greater power "God?" If not, what name do I use? In what specific ways is God more powerful than I am?

2. God knows me personally, both "who" and "what" I am.
   Discussion starters: What are three titles that define "who" I am? (Example: mother, father, homemaker, lawyer.) At my essence, "what" am I? Would changing my "who" change my "what?" Vice versa?

3. God loves me.
   Discussion starters: Respond to the idea, "God believes in you. God wants the best (health) for you." What does your thoughtful answer reveal about your concept of God?

4. My life, even with cancer, is a priceless gift.
   *Discussion starters: Respond to the idea, "A gift
   implies both a giver and requires a response of
   gratitude." What has cancer taught you
   about thankfulness?*

5. My death will be an exit from this life and an
   entrance into my next level of experience.
   *Discussion starters: What are my thoughts and
   feelings about the process of dying? About severing
   my earthly relationships?*

6. I can significantly control my quality of death by
   focusing on my quality of life.
   *Discussion starter: Share three standards to live by
   that raise the quality of your own life.*

7. I am open to the lessons of my pain and grief.
   *Discussion starter: Describe what have you
   learned about God, life, and yourself in the darkness
   of cancer?*

8. I have weighed my options and I have decided to
   prepare to live.
   *Discussion starters: Share the commitments you
   must make to begin the process of regaining your
   health. Or, to begin the process of accepting death?*

9. I love others and know that I am loved by others.
   *Discussion starters: Who do you love? Who loves
   you? Who will cherish you in their memories?
   Is this a factor which you may wish to improve
   upon - starting now?*

10. I understand that knowing God's peace is my goal and that well-being is the by-product. *Discussion starters: Describe what you understand to be the signs of God's peace. Are they present in your life? How can you cultivate greater peace?*

For the advanced wellness student

Experiencing and expressing a transcendent spiritual connection is an intentional choice. We do not have to entertain nagging suggestions about what the future may hold. Fear, uncertainty, and ambivalence need not paralyze us from living. Instead, we can choose to live now, this very moment, in spiritual humility for God's gifts of forgiveness, gratitude, and unconditional love.

Focusing on the moment may seem like classic denial, especially for those with cancer. Unless it is a mindless reaction, "living now" is not. It may be difficult to believe that this is the best time of your life. Cancer colors so much of the lens through which we see our experiences. The view can seem dark, threatening, and foreboding, as if a storm of epic proportions is on the horizon.

Yet, this is the best time of your life because it is the only time of your life. Nothing else exists but the eternal now. In the spiritual realm, yesterday and tomorrow are simply an illusion. God, and all good, is eternally present.

You have a choice: you can choose to align with God now and all that is good or you can choose to bring the past and the future into this moment. Transcendent souls align with the good in this moment.

You seek to change the pattern of your physical health. The only moment in which this can be accomplished is in the now. To do so is, ultimately, a spiritual experience. This is a big order but not impossible. It is accomplished moment to moment.

So you and I must be ever vigilant to create a state of body, mind, and spirit where we are well and live from that state. Are you treating this moment, as you read these very lines, as a brand-new moment for well-being? How can you make it new and precious and filled with health? Share your response to the following queries:

How can I express spiritual well-being, in this "now" moment? Share with the group as many ways as you can.

Two of our most powerful tools for spiritual transcendence are the power found in silence and the power of the spoken word. Our spoken word can become an affirmative claim on divine substance. Our word begins to materialize what we are asking for, what we want and what God wants for us. Our word is how we think and relate to God and God's will.

Encourage discussion and sharing regarding for what each member is praying.

Close with prayer.

Week 5

Joy Inexpressible

Getting Started

Begin with prayer.

Blessed be the God and Father of our Lord Jesus Christ! By his great mercy he has given us a new birth into a living hope through the resurrection of Jesus Christ from the dead, and into an inheritance that is imperishable, undefiled, and unfading, kept in heaven for you, who are being protected by the power of God through faith for a salvation ready to be revealed in the last time. In this you rejoice, even if now for a little while you have had to suffer various trials, so that the genuineness of your faith – being more precious than gold that, though perishable, is tested by fire – may be found to result in praise and glory and honor when Jesus Christ is revealed. Although you have not seen him, yet you love him; and even though you do not see him now, you believe in him and rejoice with an indescribable and glorious joy, for you are receiving the outcome of your faith, the salvation of your souls.
1 Peter 1:3-9 (NRSV)

This passage begins with words of praise to God, expressing thanks for the new life and new birth we have been offered through Jesus Christ. It reminds us that we have been recreated to be put in touch with eternity and eternal life. It reassures us of victory over pain, over brokenness, over our circumstances and over our poverty of hope and spirit. In it we are promised an inheritance of peace and joy which nothing can ravage or destroy and where we are untouched by the chances and changes of life. This passage doesn't pretend to say that God saves us from the troubles, problems and sorrows of life or that God sets up the trials as an obstacle to keep us down or as a test to measure our strength. But it does promise that God enables us to conquer every trouble and empowers us to strive on, to receive salvation – the deliverance from danger, disease, condemnation and brokenness.

In these words we are given the hope that we can withstand and endure anything because of what we are able to look forward to beyond the difficulty – to a magnificent inheritance, to life with God, to ultimate joy. Even the tests and trials themselves can give strength to us.

The early Christians, who suffered countless pressures, indignities, and rampant persecution, bore witness through their behavior and faith to the power and truth of the Gospel. We are encouraged to believe and bear witness too, in our own distress, in our own dilemmas and in our own disappointments throughout life. In that, we can experience God's gifts of peace and joy.

- *In what ways have you seen others exhibit joy in the midst of distress?*
- *How can you begin to see your life in a more thankful, grateful light?*
- *What difficult experiences have strengthened and blessed you?*
- *How can you use God's blessings to allow joy to inhabit your life?*

LIVE: Nurturing a Sense of Joy

Cancer takes a cumulative toll on a person's life. It is an unparalleled dilemma that threatens our personal security and erodes our sense of spontaneity. We feel angry at our misfortune and usually have ample evidence to conclude that life is unfair.

The crisis of cancer explodes many of the illusions that once anchored our lives. After being told we have cancer, it makes little difference if our home is perfectly neat and clean. Being critically ill over-rides all concern with meeting sales quotas or updating quarterly financial projections.

Cancer makes it easy for us to slip into despair. The threat is all too real; the changes rock our personal foundations. Life feels so out of control. Helplessness is often the simplest way to cope. It is not the best way.

An alternate response can lead us to a new era in our lives. This new era is characterized by joyfulness. However, it requires our intentional choice coupled with our fortitude. For in the midst of this crisis, we can learn what is important and we can act on what will be the redemptive legacy of this unwanted experience. In short, we can learn to live.

Joy, the sense of well-being evoked by an awareness that life is truly a special gift, is central to our understanding. Joy is delight in life no matter what the circumstances. Joy is personal peace coupled with a liberal sprinkling of bliss. Joy is the experience of happiness even in the face of life-threatening illness. Joy is what it means to live.

"Cancering" can be seen as a testing of our spirits. The following exercises focus on increasing our awareness of joy, the essential fortification we need in response to cancer. These queries will help you understand what you define as truly joyful and thus important.

Cultivate joy

Consider each statement. Share your level of agreement with the group. Reflect on your level of intensity surrounding each choice.

1. I am keenly aware of and appreciate my salvation and its contribution to my well-being.
   Discussion starters: Share three actions that nearly always help you feel aware of your salvation. How does that leave you joyful? Share three thought patterns that nearly always elicit pessimism and despair?

2. In seeking joy, I cultivate humor and appreciate its healing power.
   Discussion starters: What triggers my deep and genuine laughter? How might I access those moments more frequently?

3. I regularly enjoy a variety of playful activities that are both relaxing and rejuvenating.
   Discussion starters: Share ten playful activities which cost nothing. Share ten that cost under $5.00 each. Share ten playful activities that involve a partner. Share ten playful activities that involve art or culture. Share ten playful activities that involve your volunteer service to others.

4. I give and get as much touching and hugging as I need.
   Discussion starters: What "rules of displaying affection" did my family of origin live by?

*Do I practice the same as an adult? Should any
changes be made? Do I feel the freedom to be
openly expressive?*

5. I am playful in my close relationships, laughing at
   myself and others about our shared foibles.
   *Discussion starters: Share three ways positive
   playful love was expressed in your family of origin.
   Do I practice the same as an adult? Should any
   changes be made?*

6. I enjoy and affirm God's work in my life including
   my own strengths, accomplishments, and successes
   as well as those of others.
   *Discussion starters: List three examples of your
   affirmative self-talk. List three examples of your
   critical self-talk. How can you shift away from
   negative and increase the positive affirmations in
   your life?*

7. I allow myself to openly be joyful and to love.
   *Discussion starters: Share five ways you give love
   effectively and to whom. Note any expectations of
   return attached to your love-giving. How do
   you benefit from your expressions of love?*

8. I allow myself to openly receive love.
   *Discussion starters: What is the mental picture you
   hold of being loved? Where do you turn to fulfill
   that need? When human love temporarily fails you,
   how do you respond?*

9. I am able to sustain hope and joy even when cancer
    seems to dictate otherwise.
    *Discussion starters: What are your hopes? Where
    can you turn to always find a personal wellspring
    of hope? How much time do you spend in seeking
    this source?*

10. I am able to allow God's vital spirit of well-being
    to radiate from me, even when cancer would block
    that light.
    *Discussion starters: What does it mean for you to
    radiate wellness? If your wellness were a light
    bulb, how brightly is that light now shining?*

For the advanced wellness student

Cancer recovery takes appropriate downtime, moments
when we do nothing more constructive than honoring our
own needs. This does not mean a permanent retreat into
isolation and loneliness. Instead, this downtime prepares
us to live. If we deprive ourselves of this necessity, we soon
become like caged animals; at first we snarl at our family and
friends, even God. But soon we become resigned to "the
inevitable" and give in to the despair.

Advanced wellness students recognize and stop that behavior. I give you permission to claim all the downtime you
need. Create the unique feelings of joy and satisfaction that
are distinctive to your own recovery. Above all, give yourself
the necessary permission to live, laugh, and love — it's as
simple as changing a thought.

Many cancer patients have made a virtue out of deprivation.
We sacrifice for others. We constantly put our own needs

second or third. Sometimes, we've used a long-suffering stance in life to feed a false sense of our spirituality. We've served others to the point of dis-service to ourselves. In doing so, we've called ourselves "good," and at moments may have even claimed some moral superiority for these acts. Cancer is calling you to step out of that behavior. We stay there because we feel like a listless circus animal that is regularly prodded to perform. And if we perform, we receive some applause and earn our daily bread.

Come out. Live. Laugh. Love. Do not be afraid to appear selfish. Heal yourself by saying yes to your true self. Anything less is being self-destructive. Are you self-destructive? This is a very delicate question to answer with accuracy because it requires that we know something of who we really are. And that is a person whom many cancer patients have long-ago forced into the proverbial circus cage.

Who are you, really? One quick way to get a sense is to ask yourself the question:

- **What would I try if it weren't viewed as crazy by others?**

Share all you would like to do, achieve, or be if you could. If your responses look pretty exciting, even a bit "impossible", then you are on the right track. These are actually voices about living from one's true self and relying on faith in God to guide and direct your path. They are less about being selfish and more about honoring the real you and your God-given mission. I asked one of our cancer recovery classes to share their lists. Items included:

1. *Learn to waltz.*
2. *Sail the entire Mediterranean*
3. *Participate in an archeological dig.*

4. *Spend a week at a health spa.*
5. *Take voice and acting lessons.*
6. *Buy a Corvette convertible.*
7. *Locate my first true love.*
8. *Finish my college degree.*
9. *Move to Colorado.*
10. *Become a missionary in Sudan.*

Check your own list. Don't neglect this important work. Seek to understand what lies hidden within and then embrace the possibilities for making that real. Then you will achieve new levels of well-being. This is not an easy task. To help focus your imagination, complete the following prompts with the first thoughts that come to your mind:

- *The most significant lack in my life is . . .*
- *My most significant time commitment is . . .*
- *One reason I become fearful is . . .*
- *One reason I get angry is . . .*
- *One reason I feel guilty is . . .*
- *One reason I become sad is . . .*
- *As I play more, my work . . .*
- *I sometimes sabotage myself by . . .*
- *If my dreams would really come true, my family would . . .*
- *The greatest joy in my life is . . .*

One reason why this is such a difficult exercise to complete with integrity is the cultural expectations we have accepted without question. A grandmother once shared that the greatest joy in her life was her grandchildren. In the next breath she went on to tell how much she resented postponing her own activities to once again baby-sit while her daughter and son-in-law went out. Saying no to her daughter would be saying yes to herself. Unfortunately, it was a responsibility the grandmother couldn't manage. One of the central questions of healing becomes, "Are you regularly honoring your own true needs?" It definitely is not, "Am I meeting the expectations of others?" It's joy we're after. Resolve today to LIVE! One of the best ways to become more aware of our true needs is to silence our "internal critic" through a simple technique called speed writing. Here, we respond quickly to a series of prompts. And since wishes are just wishes and are allowed to be frivolous, we can feel free to express them.

As quickly as you can, finish the following phrases:

I wish _____

I wish _____

I wish _____

I especially wish _____

Wishes should frequently be taken seriously. Circle those that fall into the "take them seriously" category for you.

One of the most important things you can do for your recovery and well-being is to nurture a healthy love in your closest relationships. When all else is done, our intimate relationships help us get well, stay well, and transcend the frightening experience of cancer. Your recovery is inherently and inescapably bound to your relationships. As much as a sense of autonomy and meeting your own needs is important, they are done to facilitate your deep need to relate authentically with others. This need to give and receive love is the most basic of our heart hungers. Honor this need. Make a list of those dear ones — your inner circle of mutual caring and love.

Who are the people to whom you would most like to say, "I love you?"

To whom do you wish to say, "Thank you."

Now, before you do anything else, express your feelings to each of these people. Do so face-to-face, by phone, through a hand-written note, or e-mail. Tell them what you want them to know about your feelings toward them. Bask in the well-being. Experience the joy.

Close with Prayer

Week 6

How God Renews Health

Getting Started

Begin with prayer.

The Lord is my shepherd, I shall not want. He makes me lie
down in green pastures; he leads me beside still waters; he re-
stores my soul. He leads me in right paths for his name's sake.
Even though I walk through the darkest valley, I fear no evil; for
you are with me; your rod and your staff — they comfort me.
You prepare a table before me in the presence of my enemies; you
anoint my head with oil; my cup overflows. Surely goodness
and mercy shall follow me all the days of my life, and I shall
dwell in the house of the Lord my whole life long.
Psalm 23 (NRSV)

The preceding Psalm, 22, ends by speaking of the joy of
salvation — discovering what it means to receive the gift of
a right relationship and fellowship with God. Now, Psalm
23, expressing an individual's experience of God's grace,
describes what it feels like to be back home with God.

Using imagery with which listeners of the day would be
familiar, the psalmist talks about sheep and their relationship
to a shepherd. A good shepherd's job was to protect, direct,
shield and guide his flock. He was to provide security and
even literally lay down his life to guard the sheep that were
in danger. A sheep's existence was precarious. Weather,
wild animals and the rugged desert terrain provided particular
dangers for them. They needed the guidance and protection
of a shepherd to keep them safe and secure.

Like sheep, we too are confronted with a precarious and fragile existence. Life is not always easy or good. If we are aware of God's continuous presence in days when life goes well, we can also be certain of God when life does not go well for us. Even when we are surrounded by darkness, we can know that God provides a light along the way. Even as all of us travel through the valley of the shadow of death, we can be assured that, like a shepherd, God will be there to travel through the valley with us. Even as depression, disease, rejection and demons threaten us, God's unswerving loyalty, presence and love will pursue and provide us with reassurance every day of our lives.

- *In what ways do you need God's guidance and protection?*
- *What valleys overwhelm you and cause you to call out for help from God?*
- *Why do you think this psalm is so reassuring and comforting to so many people?*
- *How will being reassured of God's continual presence help you to begin the process of healing?*

The Awe and Wonder of Healing

A dramatic demonstration of the healing potential of the 23rd Psalm came as our cancer recovery retreat team welcomed a gentleman named Victor to one of our programs. He had metastatic liver cancer. Too weak to walk, Victor checked in to the retreat center in a wheelchair. His breathing was labored; an oxygen tank was strapped to the back of his chair and the tubes from the tank led to his nostrils. A persistent hiss could be heard from the apparatus.

Victor's skin color was ashen-gray. He was dressed in a dark blue athletic warm-up over a sweat shirt and wrapped in a heavy wool stadium blanket; he complained of being cold ever since his chemotherapy. Victor's voice was a weak and raspy whisper. He coughed often. I believed he was very close to death.

Because of his obvious need, we suspended our normal first-evening orientation and concentrated on ministering to him. After about thirty minutes of faltering attempts at communication, one of the counselors asked, "Victor, do you have a favorite verse of scripture?" His labored reply was, "The Lord is my Shepherd. I shall not want."

In what I can only describe as a divinely-inspired response, the entire group of counselors, fellow patients, and family support members - about 30 people in all - gathered around Victor, laying hands on his head, shoulders, and arms. We began to reverently repeat his favorite verse, "The Lord is my Shepherd. I shall not want."

At first, Victor had no response. But the affirmations continued, quietly, reverently, simply, person after person, "The Lord is my Shepherd. I shall not want."

Victor finally responded, silently nodding his head in agreement.

Then someone in the group said, "The Lord is my physician. I shall not want." And that was soon followed by, "The Lord is my healer. I shall not want." The tone became more positively expectant.

Victor managed to respond with a whispered, "Yes."

One of the other participants then said, "The Lord is my treatment. I shall not want." Someone else followed with, "The Lord is my source, I shall not want." And another voice affirmed, "The Lord is my health. I shall never want."

Victor's posture became more upright; he became more alert. He smiled and said with a clearer and stronger voice, "I shall never want." You could discern the emphasis he placed on the word 'never.'

As these affirmations, all derived from the first sentences of the 23rd Psalm, continued, we experienced what I can only call a miracle, actually several miracles. A woman participant, whom we later learned was suffering with painful neuropathy following chemotherapy, began to weep uncontrollably. She sobbed and then moaned and loudly groaned. She collapsed to the floor and was supported and held by another woman who simply kept repeating, "The Lord is our Shepherd. We shall not want." The moaning continued; it was painful just to hear the sounds that originated from deep within the woman's body and spirit.

Victor's color seemed to be improving.

Another woman, wearing a turban that covered her chemotherapy-induced baldness, stood with hands outstretched over her head and began repeating, "Lord, you are my healing. I shall never want." Soon a group of five or six was gathered around her, hands held upward, affirming with her, "Lord, you are my healing. I shall never want."

Victor unwrapped himself from the blanket. He was perspiring.

I hesitate to report all this because I am deeply suspicious of healing theatrics. Yet, as much as I did not, and still do not, seek this type of emotionalism, something other-worldly was obviously at work here.

Victor leaned forward and stood up, directly in front of his wheelchair. He was tall and thin, yet he now had a whole new persona. And, in one of only two times I have seen a personal aura — the luminous energy field that is believed to emanate from living beings — Victor was surrounded by a glowing light.

I stood back in awe, even fear, and watched the light around Victor change from a purple to an orange to a golden yellow to a bright white. I was later to learn that I was one of only two people who saw it. Not even Victor realized its presence. It disturbed me that everyone did not see it. Was I hallucinating? I can only report it was very real.

The large room became silent. The woman who had been sobbing and moaning was now quiet, her energy spent. She was held and prayed for by several people. The group that surrounded the turban-clad woman was now embraced in a huddle of fifteen or more people. Several of us just stood by in wonder.

It was Victor who finally spoke, "I think I have been healed." We stood by expressing amazement and gratitude.

I do not pretend to fully understand what happened that evening. And in the few occasions when I have shared this experience with others who claim to be experts in this field, the explanations leave me wanting. Victor, in his annual Hanukkah letter, referred to it briefly by saying, "When I acknowledged God as my complete Source, I was healed." I understand that explanation. It is present in many healing experiences. I also understand that we have incomplete knowledge of healing. Experiences like this defy modern science and certainly challenge conventional thinking. Yet, they are integral to the experiences of thousands of people who are healed. I welcome the fact that we are now able to share these experiences without the fear of clinical dismissal or theological condemnation.

This I also understand. There is a power within us. It is within you just as surely as it is within me. I believe this power is responsive to our highest needs. When we make conscious connection with this power, it literally transforms our lives because in our true nature, we are this power in expression.

You and I live by and in the gift of God's goodness. We do not have to entertain the nagging thoughts of fear that create dis-ease. Even in the midst of cancer, especially in the midst of cancer, I encourage you to acknowledge God as your complete source. Become consciously aware of that powerful connection. Therein is found God's peace. Therein is healing of the highest order.

Discussion starters: What did Victor experience? Is that available for you and me?

The 23rd Psalm Prescription

Read the 23rd Psalm five times a day for thirty days:
Dose 1: *First thing upon awakening in the morning. Read it carefully and meditatively.*
Dose 2: *Immediately after breakfast. It is not to be taken quickly or hurriedly.*
Dose 3: *Immediately after lunch. Take your time. Think about each phrase.*
Dose 4: *Again after dinner. Give your mind time to absorb the meaning.*
Dose 5: *The very last thing before you go to sleep. Pray on its meaning.*

Take this prescription exactly as prescribed, and in thirty days a new and powerful way of living will be firmly implanted in your mind and spirit. Thank God for the renewal in your health and your life.

Close with a dose of the 23rd Psalm Perscription.

Week 7

A Pastor's Perspective
Nothing Can Seperate
Us from God

Getting Started

Begin with prayer.

What then are we to say about these things? If God is for us, who is against us? He who did not withhold his own Son, but gave him up for all of us, will he not with him also give us everything else? Who will bring any charge against God's elect? It is God who justifies. Who is to condemn? It is Christ Jesus, who died, yes, who was raised, who is at the right hand of God, who indeed intercedes for us. Who will separate us from the love of Christ? Will hardship, or distress, or persecution, or famine, or nakedness, or peril, or sword? ... No, in all these things we are more than conquerors through him who loved us. For I am convinced that neither death, nor life, nor angels, nor rulers, nor things present, nor things to come, nor powers, nor height, nor depth, nor anything else in all creation, will be able to separate us from the love of God in Christ Jesus our Lord.
Romans 8:31-35, 37-39 (NRSV)

One of the most poetic, lyrical and eloquent passages in the Bible, these words of the Apostle Paul reach out to encourage us with a message of comfort and assurance. Its undeniable theme asks: if God is willing to grant the gift of himself through Jesus Christ to us, is there anything then that God would withhold from us? It tells us we can trust a loyalty and love like that for anything we need. It tells us God is interceding for us and therefore we are safe. It tells us while God is the only power that can condemn us; God is in fact the very one who protects us. It means if the only potential accuser is actually our benefactor, then truly we have nothing to fear from anything or anyone. It means there are no afflictions, no hardships, no perils, no powers, no malign influences or forces, no pains and no threats in the entire world that can separate us from God and God's love.

Through these words, we are assured that gone forever is reason to give in to the temptation that assumes misfortune is evidence of God's rejection or disfavor. These words banish once and for all the temptation to conclude that when things go badly, it means God has deserted us. These words reassure us that God *is* for us. They reassure us that nothing significant can therefore be against us. There is no dimension of reality we can imagine — no matter how frightening, lonely or daunting — that has the power to frustrate God's care and love for us. There is no creaturely power that can affect our lives in any but a temporary way. And even our nearly limitless ability to rebel against God is overcome and we are saved from our last and greatest enemy, ourselves. Through these words we are assured of grace, which is the basis of our confidence. Suffering and affliction do not mean God has abandoned us. They are not God's last word, as the resurrection of Christ has demonstrated. God's love is power enough to overcome all obstacles, power enough to spare us and help us overcome even ourselves. This passage makes it very clear that Christians heed and obey God by God's own grace rather than by some power of our own. We indeed are conquerors because of the love, grace and goodness of God.

- *How have you ever felt separated, abandoned or forgotten by God?*
- *Is there anything in your life that reminds you that God has not forsaken you?*
- *What do you need to reassure you that you can conquer your difficulties?*
- *How have you already conquered difficulties and potential defeats in your life?*

Understanding What We Believe

More Than Conquerors

At the heart of the Judeo-Christian message is the promise of triumph. Throughout the scriptures there is woven a constant and distinct thread, declaring God's unwavering, eternal, gracious love. That love consistently overcomes and conquers all the brokenness, distress, disappointment, disease and hatred of the world. It never leaves. It never ends. It never is taken away. In spite of the unfaithfulness of the very first humans, the mistakes of the patriarchs and matriarchs, the disobedience of the judges and monarchs, the failure of the nations to pay heed to God's prophets and messengers, the arrogance of the leaders who challenged Christ, and the divisiveness and contentiousness of those in the early church, God never forsakes or gives up on humanity. In spite of all the evils that threaten and tempt the people of the world, God always finds a way to help, to heal and to offer new life to those who are beleaguered and beaten down.

When God's people experience the indignities of exile from their homes and one another, over and over again, God works to restore and reunite them. When God's people wander without apparent aim or purpose, over and over again, God acts to guide and accompany them. When God's people fall into patterns of destruction and deceit, over and over again, God gives them examples of justice and mercy to show them a better way. When God's people break under the burden of illness and human limitation, over and over again, God reaches out to revive and renew them. In all these things and countless more, God intercedes, over and over again, to help, to save, to restore and revive the people — making us more than conquerors over all that rises up to bring us down.

In 1779, John Newton wrote some of the most beloved and inspiring words the last few centuries have known. As his very life was threatened by a violent storm while he sailed at sea, Newton came to understand and comprehend how much God loved him and wanted him to overcome the brokenness in his life. Newton's mother died when he was only six years of age. He had only two years of formal schooling. He longed to join his father as a sailor, and did at age 11. But Newton's dreams turned to nightmares. His father rejected him. He clashed with his employers and ended up in jail. His life was marked by debauchery. The ships on which he sailed brought people into slavery. At age 39, facing his mortality and his emptiness, John Newton survived the storm and allowed his life to be turned around. He triumphed over his past and conquered his demons. The understanding of his triumph is conveyed in these confident words:

Through many dangers, toils, and snares, I have already come; 'tis grace hath brought me safe thus far, and grace will bring me home.
The Lord has promised good to me, his word my hope secures; he will my shield and portion be, as long as life endures.

God has promised goodness to us and God has delivered on the promise. Through every age of time, including our own, God has used people — seemingly broken, apparently defeated, certainly suffering and obviously threatened — to conquer and restore them to a triumphant life. Through them — through us — God reminds all the world of the renewing power and the re-creative possibility inherent in our faith.

In the nearly 20 years in which I have been a parish pastor, I have known countless persons who have faced the realities of cancer. Nearly all have been persons of abiding faith. But some have seriously doubted and questioned the existence of a God of goodness and love. And then, a remarkable few have possessed extraordinary depth and conviction in their walk with God. Pastors are accorded access along the journey of living that is singularly unique. We are so often intimately involved in times of trouble *and* in times of celebration. We are witness to some of the worst of human behavior and experience *and* to some of the very best of what humans can be and do. We regularly hear of the deep struggles *and* of the still longed-for dreams of those within our realm of care. A diagnosis of cancer nearly always brings with it long periods of time that force patients and their families to focus with laser intensity on its ramifications and cure. Those of us who are in such close and intimate connection with them frequently accompany them through significant moments along the way.

Inevitably, as I have shared in the journey, as I have sat by their bedsides at home or in a hospital, as I have prayed with them for strength and comfort, as I have visited with them while they received chemotherapy, as I have listened in their living rooms and their kitchens as they told their stories, as I have rejoiced with them as they were given the news that all signs of the disease were gone or — at times — as I have held their hands as they lay dying, a few undeniable truths were inevitable and clear: every one of those living with cancer and faith ministered to me and to many others around them and in spite of the struggles that all of them went through, there was triumph involved in every one of their lives.

I was privileged and blessed to witness those who took their diagnosis and determined that it would reprioritize their lives in significant, positive and purposeful ways. They would waste less time, speak out more, become involved in deeper ways within pursuits meaningful to them, be less afraid or resolve to mend brokenness. They would renew their faith and reconnect with God, vowing to share, care, and forgive in new and different ways. They would reach out to strengthen relationships and to bridge the separation that our lives so often create. They would cast aside the aspects of their lives that they realized were not of value or affirming of life. They would seek and find a peace that passed conventional understanding, a peace which lifted them above the temporal ways of this world. They would strive to live with cancer and not die from it. They would choose to live their lives with greater abundance and deeper thanksgiving, seeing each day and moment as a blessing to be savored and used with care. They would feel more joy and appreciate everyday experiences and gestures in passionate new ways. They would teach all those around them who were willing to learn that in spite of the challenges upon them, they could live — and die if necessary — in a triumphant, courageous way. That way is God's way. It is God's hope for us in this life and in the next.

God's undeniable will, as seen over and over again in the scriptures, is for us to be in connection and communion with God, to experience the divine and to receive eternity. God is constantly working to give us new chances, new opportunities, to find triumph and victory. God is continually reaching out to infuse humanity with a better and more satisfying way to live and move and have our being. God did it through the aged Abraham and Sarah, giving them progeny and a legacy when they doubted they could ever have either. God did it through David, making him the most successful king Israel knew, even though he was duplicitous, an adulterer and self-serving. God did it through Israel itself, delivering the nation many times from oppression, defeat, division and self-inflicted turmoil. God did it through Christ, who touched those who were previously untouchable, who brought mercy to those who were previously unforgivable and who shared love with those who were previously unlovable. God did it through the Apostle Paul, a hater, enemy and persecutor of the early Christians, who was converted to be the greatest follower and voice for Christ the world has ever known. Through the Apostle Paul, God continues to do it by reminding us in Romans Eight that nothing this world can do to us or throw at us can separate us from the love of God. We are more than conquerors because of all these triumphs, and so many more.

H. G. Spafford was a successful Chicago businessman, who bid his wife and four daughters goodbye in 1873 as they left to sail on the French steamer Ville de Havre for a visit with relatives in Europe. He didn't know at the time that he would never see his daughters alive again. While crossing the Atlantic, their ship collided with another ship, the Lochearn, and sank within 30 minutes, taking the Spafford's daughters with it. Mrs. Spafford survived. But nearly everyone else on board died, 226 people in all. Grieving, Mr. Spafford sailed to Europe to be with his wife and was moved to put his feelings into words as his ship passed over the site of his daughters' drownings. His faith told him that in spite of this terrible tragedy, triumph could be experienced and life could go on. Three years later his poetic words were put to music and we were given another beloved and inspiring hymn of assurance and promise:

When peace like a river, attendeth my way,
When sorrows like sea billows roll;
Whatever my lot, thou hast taught me to say,
It is well, it is well with my soul.
It is well with my soul,
it is well, it is well with my soul.

The testimonies of those who have suffered and lost, of those who have been burdened and beaten down, of those who have faced fear and countless demons, and yet, who have found a way to rise above and live beyond all that has come, can be of true hope and assurance to us through our own struggles and grief.

Cancer is a struggle for which there are not enough words to describe all the feelings, fears, frustrations and moments fraught with anxiety it brings. It clearly changes lives. Those changes certainly bring a new perception of life and its meaning. Sometimes those changes are positive and good. Sometimes those changes break us apart and embitter us in terrible ways. But they do not have to. Our faith reminds us, over and over again, how God lifts us up, carries us through, delivers us to a better life - both here on earth and with God for all eternity. Our faith reminds us that nothing —no evil power, no painful existence, no cancer — can ultimately separate us from the love of God in Christ Jesus, the Lord of life, the Lord of love, the Lord of hope, the Lord of triumph. We are more than conquerors because of that.

Encourage further sharing among your group. Discuss if you would like to continue these meetings. If so, see the next section, "How to Organize & lead or a Cancer Support Group."

Close with prayer.

Resources

David F. Payne, **Daily Study Bible Series: I and II Samuel** *(Philadelphia: The Westminster Press, 1982)*

William Barclay, **Daily Study Bible Series: The Gospel of Mark, Revised Edition** *(Philadelphia: The Westminster Press, 1975)*

Lamar Williamson, Jr., **Interpretation: Mark, A Bible Commentary for Teaching and Preaching** *(Louisville: John Knox Press, 1983)*

Madeleine S. and J. Lane Miller, **The New Harper's Bible Dictionary, Revised** *(San Francisco: Harper and Row Publishers, 1973)*

William H. Gentz, General Editor, **The Dictionary of Bible and Religion** *(Nashville: Abingdon, 1986)*

William Barclay, **Daily Study Bible Series: The Letters of James and Peter,** *Revised Edition (Philadelphia: The Westminster Press, 1976)*

Pheme Perkins, **Interpretation: I and II Peter, James and Jude, A Bible Commentary for Teaching and Preaching** *(Louisville: John Knox Press, 1995)*

William Barclay, **Daily Study Bible Series: The Gospel of Matthew, Revised Edition, Vol. 1** *(Philadelphia: The Westminster Press, 1975)*

Douglas R. A. Hare, **Interpretation: Matthew, A Bible Commentary for Teaching and Preaching** *(Louisville: John Knox Press, 1993)*

George A. F. Knight, **Daily Study Bible Series: Psalms Vol. 1** *(Philadelphia: The Westminster Press, 1982)*

William Barclay, **Daily Study Bible Series: Letters to the Romans, Revised Edition** *(Philadelphia: The Westminster Press, 1975)*

Paul Achtemeier, **Interpretation: Romans, A Bible Commentary for Teaching and Preaching** *(Louisville: John Knox Press, 1985)*

Ernest K. Emurian, **Hymn Stories for Programs** *(Grand Rapids: Baker Book House, 1963)*

Nathanael Olson, **Hymns of Faith** *(Milwaukee: Ideals Publishing Company, 1975)*

How to Organize and Lead a Cancer Support Group

INTRODUCTION

This handbook presents the fundamental aspects of successful cancer support group leadership. It also includes ideas of cancer support group organizers and participants, as well as a comparison of discussion versus debate and an application to register local groups with the Cancer Recovery Foundation's international network.

The cancer-based support group is a simple and powerful method for learning about health and well-being. It is based on the experiences and knowledge of group members as opposed to individual experts. It expands horizons by insuring that a variety of views are given consideration.

The cancer support group leader is critical to the success of the group efforts. This person does not "teach" in the usual sense of the word. A cancer support group leader does not have to be an expert on the subject being discussed. Instead, he or she must have enough familiarity with the subject to be able to raise views that have not been considered by the group. The leader's central task is to create an atmosphere for exploration, one in which each participant feels at ease in expressing ideas and responding to those of others.

A cancer support group is democracy in action. It requires a leader who can give focus and at the same time encourage group ownership of the discussion. Cancer support group leaders come from a variety of backgrounds and many may have had no formal training in discussion leadership. Whether the leader has the opportunity to participate in a training program or simply jumps into the role of cancer support group leader, the attitude that best serves the group is one of constantly honing discussion-enhancing skills.

So let's get started, let's be underway. It's time to consider how to start and lead a successful cancer support group.

What is a cancer support group?

In Dallas, a dozen people are comfortably seated around the living room on a Thursday evening. In the Los Angeles area, over 20 people are gathered in a classroom in one of America's largest churches. In Baltimore, eight co-workers meet over lunch on a monthly basis.

Look at all the groups and you'll see one person speaking, several others looking like they would like to make a point, another person consulting a notebook, and still others listening attentively. This is a cancer support group in action.

In a cancer support group, groups of people ranging in size from five to 25, meet regularly to discuss ideas and activities based on the concepts of healing and wellness. Some groups may be focused on maintaining health and well-being. Others are devoted to recovery. Mutual support is apparent in all.

The length of each cancer support group session varies. A lunch-time group at a major college in Florida is limited to 45 minutes, twice a month. A hospital-based cancer support group meets weekly for two hours.

Each group is lead by a person whose role is simply to aid in a lively but focused discussion. Participants receive, in advance, reading materials covering the topics for the session. Most of the assignments are from a book or workbook.

Two individuals, the organizer and the leader, are central to the creation and success of a cancer support group. The organizer selects or develops the course material, recruits participants, arranges the logistics of the meetings, and chooses the discussion leader. The discussion leader stimulates and moderates the group and guides it towards exploring each subject and supporting one another.

Cancer support groups are a well-tested, practical, and effective method for adults to learn about self-care as supportive of conventional medical care. Cancer support groups are voluntary, informal, democratic, and highly participatory. Cancer support groups engage their participants in health and well-being concerns, and bring the wisdom of ordinary people to bear on the issues. Cooperation and participation are valued and encouraged so that the group can capitalize on the experience of each of its members.

All viewpoints are taken seriously in a cancer support group. Each person is guaranteed the opportunity to participate. But central to the group is the covenant that one person's ideas need not be, should not be, forced on another. What is right for one person's recovery may not be correct for another. The cancer support group belongs to its participants. Individual members ultimately set the agenda and control the content of the discussions. The process — a democratic discussion among equals — is as important as the content. The goal of a cancer support group is not to impart knowledge in order to make participants into experts, but rather to deepen their understanding and judgment by focusing on the key value of personal accountability. The reading material and discussion may present a variety of viewpoints; the group leader encourages the expression of all personal views and experiences. The group works through difficult issues and grapples with a variety of choices. Common ground is sought in the end but a consensus or compromise is not necessary. It all goes toward supporting each individual's decision on how best to create wellness for him or herself.

Almost any organization can offer a cancer support group to educate and empower its members. In companies, churches, civic community groups, non-profit organizations, government entities, labor unions, and even individual houses, both patient and family members can profit from this small-group support effort.

A cancer support group will provide benefits for the participants as well as the sponsoring organization. The participants gain knowledge, move toward higher levels of well-being, and have a rewarding personal experience. For the sponsoring organization, a cancer support group represents a valuable opportunity for health promotion, disease prevention, and life enrichment. Participation in a cancer support group may often increase co-workers' commitment to an organization. And in a era of increasingly rapid rises in healthcare costs, cancer support groups may also benefit the organization by providing direct healthcare cost savings.

There are endless variations to the basic format for a cancer support group. The most common structure is for a cancer support group to meet once a month for at least ten months a year. Others may meet weekly for a shorter period of time. And while regular weekly discussions usually produce better results, other schedules can also work very well.

Some cancer support groups combine their work with an organization's regular monthly meeting. But even for those groups that cannot meet regularly, a workshop format can be used at a conference or a retreat center with the entire subject matter being treated over a period of one or two days.

In addition to video tapes or audio tapes, a variety of printed matter is used. Small-group activities and exercises are included by some cancer support groups to add diversity to the sessions. A limited amount of homework is not uncommon.

The strength of the cancer support group is its flexibility. Every group situation is unique and cancer support group organizers are encouraged to always adapt the basic format to their communities and organizations.

Overview of a Typical Cancer Support Group

What follows is an outline for a single cancer support group session. While there are variations of this theme, it is helpful to consider this as your roadmap. You may wish to have this handy for reference as you lead your own cancer support group.

(1) INTRODUCTIONS

Begin your session by giving the group members the opportunity to briefly introduce themselves. If you've already met several times, at least go around the room to give names.

(2) GROUND RULES

Remind everyone of the ground rules for cancer support groups. These include:

(a) *We meet to explore ideas that enhance health and enrich life.*

(b) *The ideas are meant to support, not replace, medical care.*

(c) *The role of the leader is to keep the discussion focused and moving forward.*

(d) *The role of the participants is to share beliefs, insights, and concerns and to listen carefully to others.*

(e) *The ideas expressed do not necessarily represent those of the organization or its affiliates. The views are those of each individual participant.*

(f) *Be willing to examine your own beliefs in light of what others say.*

(g) *Help assure that each participant has the opportunity to share and that no one person dominates the discussion.*

(h) *Put-downs or personal attacks will not be tolerated.*

(i) *Seek everyone's agreement with these ground rules.*

(3) LAY OUT THE RANGE OF VIEWS

If the resource material you are using lays out well-defined and distinct views on the subject, this part will be straightforward. One useful way to make sure all the views are adequately presented is to ask for a brief explanation of each view from different members of the group.

If the subject matter needs more definition, you might divide the participants into assigned groups and give each one the task of preparing a brief overview of the best possible case for one of the views. This exercise helps make sure that a variety of ideas will be considered in the discussion. Make it clear that this is just a way to give each view a fair hearing and that this isn't yet the time for an open discussion of the views.

(4) DISCUSSION

This part of the cancer support group is devoted to wide-open discussion. Encourage participants to explore their own beliefs as opposed to those who might have been assigned a given subject for presentation. One useful way to proceed is to ask group members to comment on what they find appealing and unappealing about the various views that have been put on the on the table for discussion. The leader might ask, "Do you find yourself more in agreement with or a critic of that view? Why?" If the group neglects a major point of view, the group leader should raise it for consideration and ask, "What are the concerns that underlie this view?"

(5) SUMMARY

Ask participants to summarize the most important insights of their discussion. "Do any common concerns emerge?" "In what ways do you see the issue differently as a result of considering new views?" Participants will likely have some common concerns and goals even though they may have different ideas about how to address or achieve them.

(6) EVALUATION

End by asking participants for their thoughts and analysis on the group process. What did they like or dislike about the discussion? You may wish to ask for this in writing to give participants the opportunity to respond anonymously. If you will be meeting again, remind the group of the topic and assignment, if any, for the next session. If this is your last session in a series, give participants the opportunity to discuss how they might continue to be involved in this issue. Ask for suggestions for continuing topics.

Tips for Effective Discussion Leadership

Be prepared. The leader does not need to be an expert, or even the most knowledgeable person in the group, on the topic being discussed. However, the leader should be the best prepared for the discussion. This means understanding the goals of the cancer support group, familiarity with the subject, thinking ahead of time about the directions in which the discussion might go, and preparation of discussion questions to aid the group in considering the subject. Preparation enables you to give your full attention to group dynamics and to what individuals in the group are saying.

Set a relaxed and open tone. Welcome everyone and create a non-judgmental atmosphere. Well-placed humor is always welcomed. Help people focus on the ideas rather than the personalities.

Establish clear ground rules. Know that you are seeking to have agreement on the previously stated ground rules. Ask participants if they agree with them. Ask if they wish to add anything. Cancer-based support groups operate best when group members are encouraged to express and reflect their honest opinions. This implies that all views should be respected. Though disagreement and conflict about the ideas can be useful, disagreement should not, must not, be personal. Put-downs, name-calling, labeling, or personal attacks simply will not be tolerated. It is critical to hear from everyone who wishes to speak. People who tend to speak frequently in groups should make a special effort to allow others the opportunity to speak. The role of the leader is to remain neutral and to guide the conversation according to the ground rules.

Be constantly aware of the group process. Always use your "third eye" to monitor the group flow. You're not only helping to keep the group focused on the content of the discussion, but you will be monitoring how well the participants are communicating with each other. This means being constantly aware of who has spoken, who hasn't spoken, and whose points haven't yet received a fair hearing. Consider splitting up into smaller groups to examine a variety of viewpoints or to give people a chance to talk more easily and openly about their personal connection with the issue.

Some practical insights for leaders include:
- *When wrestling with when to intervene, err on the side of non-intervention.*
- *Do not talk after each comment or answer every question. Allow the participants to respond directly to each other. The most effective leaders often say little, but are constantly thinking about how to move the group towards its goal.*
- *Don't be afraid of silence. It will sometimes take a while for someone to offer an answer to a question you pose.*
- *Don't let anyone dominate. Ask the quiet ones, "What is your opinion on this issue?"*

* *Remember that a cancer support group is not a debate but a discussion. If participants slip into the debate mode, don't hesitate to ask the group to help re-establish the ground rules. It's as simple as saying "Help me, group. Are we into a debate or a discussion? What are our ground rules?"*

Grapple with the content. Seek to have the group consider a wide range of views. Ask the group to think about the advantages and disadvantages of different ways of approaching an issue or solving a problem. In this way the trade-offs involved in making tough choices become clear.

Ask the participants to think about the concerns and the values that underlie each choice. For example, if someone is debating on whether to proceed with conventional medical care, ask them, "What is the evidence that makes you believe this is a viable option?" "What beliefs would you have to change in order to consider an alternative intervention?"

Do not allow the group to focus or be overly influenced by one particular personal experience. Summarize the discussion occasionally, or encourage a group member to do so, and then move on. As the leader, you must remain neutral about the content and be cautious about expressing your own values. If you must express a value, label it as such. Then help participants identify "common ground." But never try to force a consensus of opinion.

Use questions skillfully. Some of the most effective discussion questions for cancer support groups include:

* *What seems to be the key point here?*
* *What is the crux of your disagreement?*
* *What would like to add to (or support, or challenge) that point?*

- *Could you give an example or describe a personal experience to illustrate that point?*
- Could you help us understand the reasoning behind your opinion?
- What experiences or beliefs might lead rational and caring people to support this point of view?
- What do you think people who hold that opinion care deeply about?
- What would be a strong case against what you just said?
- What do you find most persuasive about this point of view?
- What is it about this position that you simply cannot live without?
- Are there any points on which most of us would agree?

Reserve time to close the discussion. Ask the group for closing comments and thoughts about the subject matter of the session. You may wish to ask participants to share any new ideas or insights that they have received as a result of the discussion. Remember, you are not seeking consensus. The most common close will be, "Some people think this about the subject matter and others believe differently."

If you will be meeting again, remind the group of the readings and subject for the next session, as well as time and place for meeting. Thank everyone for their contributions. Provide time for the group to evaluate the process, either through sharing aloud or through brief written evaluations.

After the group has completed, make it clear that ongoing one-on-one discussions and sharing are very much encouraged. This is often the time when specific issues, which may have limited interest or application to the group, are shared in more depth. Here is where the personal experience of one participant can directly benefit the personal concerns of another.

How to Handle a Problem

Most cancer support groups go smoothly because participants are there voluntarily and have ownership in the program. But there are challenges in any group process. What follows are some of the typical difficulties that a cancer support group leader will encounter along with some possible ways to deal with these difficulties.

Problem: Some participants don't say anything and seem shy.

Possible Responses: Draw out the quiet participants, without putting them on the spot, first by making eye contact. Smile. It reminds them that you would like to hear from them. Be aware of the non-verbal cues to see if they want to speak. Frequently, people will feel more comfortable in later sessions of a cancer support group. Feeling more comfortable, they will begin to participate. When someone does come forward with a brief comment, after staying in the background for most of the session, you can encourage him or her by conveying genuine interest and asking for more information. Speaking with people before and after the session is always helpful. As the leader, you create the open environment.

Problem: An aggressive person dominates the discussion.

Possible Response: As the group leader, it is your responsibility to restrain domineering participants. Once it becomes clear what this person is doing, you must intervene and set limits. Fail to do so and the group will invariably disintegrate. Start by reminding the dominating person that you want to hear from all members of the support group. Next, you might ask him or her not to talk until everyone else has had a chance to speak. Interrupt if necessary: "Bill, we've heard from you, now let's hear what Alice has to say." If a participant goes into a lengthy digression, you must interrupt: "Jane, we are wandering off the subject. Please make your point now." Or, "Ralph, I am now going to repeat back to you what I believe I heard you say. Tell me briefly where I am wrong."

Problem: Lack of focus, the group not moving forward or participants wander off the topic.

Possible Response: Responding to these issues can be a gray area. After all, the discussion belongs to the group members. Yet, it is the leader's job to help the group stay with the subject at hand.

The leader must give some leeway to participants who want to explore closely-related topics. However, if only a few participants are carrying the discussion in a new direction, the others in the group will almost always feel frustrated, resentful, and bored. The leader must refocus the discussion. One effective way to do this is by asking, "How does your point relate to today's topic?" Another way might be, "That's an interesting point, but I would suggest we return to the central issue of today's discussion."

Now, here is the gray area. If most or all participants are more interested in pursuing a different topic than the planned one, perhaps one that has just become prominent in current events, the leader should be sensitive to that and bring it to the group's attention. But allow the group to have a chance to reconsider the topic in their goals for the session. Give it to the group for the decision; do not let it happen by accident.

Problem: A participant gives mis-information which you know to be false. Or, participants get hung up in a dispute about facts, but no one present knows the answer.

Possible Response: Your most important question in this situation is to ask, "Has anyone heard of conflicting information?" If no one offers a correction, gently offer one yourself. If no one knows the facts, and the point is not essential, put it aside and move on. If the point is central to the discussion, encourage group members to look up the information before the next meeting. Remind the group that experts often disagree, and there may be no generally accepted answer.

Problem: Lack of interest, no excitement, no one wants to talk, only a few people are participating.

Possible Response: This does not happen often in cancer support groups, but it may occur if the leader talks too much or does not give participants enough time to respond after posing questions. People need time to think, reflect and get ready to speak up.

When no one wants to talk, remember this helpful tool: Pose a question and go around the group so that everyone has a chance to respond. For example, "What is your opinion on the mind/body connection to this point?"

Occasionally, you will have a group of people who are tired or who have had a bad day. Or, the lack of excitement in the discussion may be that the group seems to be in agreement and isn't coming to grips with the tensions inherent in the issue. In either case, the leader's job is to try to bring other views into the discussion, especially if no one in the group holds them. Try, "Do you know people who hold other beliefs?" "What would they see as the strongest criticism of the views we have expressed?"

Problem: Tension or open conflict in the group. Perhaps two participants begin to argue. Or, a participant gets angry, yells at another, or puts another person down.

Possible Response: When there is tension, address it directly. Get it out in the open with a comment like, "We have an obvious difference of opinion here." Explain that, for conflict to be productive, it needs to remain focused on the issues. This means that it is acceptable to challenge someone's ideas, but it is not acceptable to challenge them personally. You must boldly interrupt personal attacks, name calling, or put-downs as soon as they occur. You will be better able to do so if you establish the ground rules that disallow such behaviors and encourage tolerance for all views. Don't hesitate to appeal to the group for help. If the group members bought into the ground rules, they will support you.

Responsibilities of the Organizer

The cancer support group organizer is the creator of the cancer support group. The organizer selects the subject matter and material that provides the framework and the substance for the discussions. In some cases, this subject may already have been done by the program's sponsoring organization.

The cancer support group organizer also recruits participants, chooses the cancer support group discussion leader, and attends to all the logistical details surrounding the group's meetings. The organizer sets the tone for the program and must convey its purpose and goals to both the leader and to the participants.

The most successful cancer support groups are involved with an existing organization from which participants can be drawn. These typically include a hospital, a business, a federal, state, or municipal organization, or a church. If you have organized a public program or a group activity of any kind, you can organize a cancer support group. There is no one model for organizing a cancer support group. Shape the program to meet the needs of the sponsoring group and the participants. While the following suggestions are appropriate for most situations, special circumstances may call the modifications. Customization should be encouraged.

Select The Reference Material

The most successful cancer support groups have a set of reference materials that is adaptable to their purpose. Often this is a book, but these materials may also include videos, readings, magazine articles and other wellness-based resources. Cancer Recovery Foundation produces a wide variety of materials. Contact the Foundation for full information.

As the organizer, you will want to make the material more interesting and useful to the members of your cancer support group. This is easily done by:

* *Adding discussion questions that emphasize the way the subject matter affects your community or organization.*
* *Supplementing the base reference material with articles from newspapers, newsletters, or the Internet.*
* *Asking participants to bring and share relevant, current clippings.*
* *Contacting people in your community — teachers, public officials, medical authorities — who are experts in the area and my be able to share materials.*

(NOTE: It is not recommended that you bring in local experts as an authority to make a presentation. While they may be invited as a group member, putting them in the authority role negates the patient empowerment of cance support groups.)

Remember, the reference material is important. However, great cancer support groups do not require original or top-quality, professional-looking resources. The key ingredients of a successful cancer support group are the leader's skills and the participants' energy and commitment to the program.

Recruiting Participants

Your personal contact is the single key to successful recruiting. Invitations are most effective when they are made on a personal basis. The key is to convey to the potential participant that they have unique contributions to make to the discussions. Be sure to explain the goals of the cancer support group, and ask people to make a commitment to attend each session. They're doing this not only for the sake of continuity, but also to create a high level of social support and comfort within the group.

Even if the initial response is small, it is better to begin the cancer support group rather than to wait for more people to sign up. Ask those who are present to invite three other people to the next session. Try to get publicity in the local media or your organization's newsletter. Once the cancer support group is rolling, others are likely to hear about it and become interested.

Select A Leader

As the organizer, choosing the leader may be your most important decision. A poor leader will ruin a cancer support group and a good one will make it a wonderful and exciting experience. The most important consideration in selecting a leader should be his or her skill and experience in leading discussions. Try to assess how a person would handle the most difficult aspects of leading a support group. The key: would he or she keep the discussion focused? Could he or she draw out the quiet people? Could he or she restrain the aggressive participants without alienating them?

If the person you are considering for the role of cancer support group leader has not been part of a training program, you will need to describe your goals and explain how a cancer support group works. Be sure to share a copy of this handbook with your potential discussion leader.

Organize The Meetings

Place is important. Find a meeting room that has minimal distractions and where participants can chat informally both before and after the sessions. Someone's living room or a meeting room in an office or church can all be appropriate places.

The organizer must decide — preferably with input from the participants — on the date and time for the sessions. Most groups choose evening sessions. However, workplace wellness groups are finding either lunch hour or early mornings to be convenient. Polling half of your participants will give you the date and time answers you seek.

Part of your organizational responsibilities are to assure that the reading material is received by the participants several days in advance of the first session. You should also distribute ahead of time any introductory material about

about your cancer support group or about the sponsoring organization.

As the organizer, you should start each session with a very brief introduction of the subject matter and the leader. The leader will then do the welcoming and facilitate the session's start. Your task is simply to set the stage for the leader. Your personal endorsement of the leader's strengths and abilities goes far to instill everyone's confidence.

Seek Feedback

Once the cancer support group begins, the organizer's role becomes secondary to the leader's role. However, the organizer is in the best position to provide feedback to the leader. Most cancer support groups are based on multi-session programs. Conduct an evaluation at the end of the second meeting, or at least at the half-way point. Of course, you will want to give an opportunity for feedback after the final session. As the organizer, you will also be taking part in the cancer support group. Be available before and after the sessions and ask for input about any problem. Help the leader correct the issues before the next session.

The Role of the Participant

The goal of a cancer support group is not to learn a lot of facts, or to obtain group consensus. Rather, it is to deepen each person's understanding of the issue. This can occur in a focused discussion when people exchange views freely and consider a variety of viewpoints. But it happens only if we pay attention to the process. A democratic discussion among equals is the key to the process. This process is as important as the content.

The following points are intended to help participants in a cancer support group to make the most of this experience.

Notice the ways in which you can help the group as well as yourself.

1. *Listen carefully to others. Make certain you give every person the opportunity to speak.*

2. *Maintain an open mind. In a cancer support group you do not score points by sticking rigidly to early statements. This is a safe place where you can feel free to explore ideas that you may have failed to consider, or ever rejected, in the past.*

3. *Seek first to understand. Your own knowledge of any subject matter is not complete until you understand other points of view and why people feel that way. It is critical to respect the people who disagree with you. In fact, you should strive to be able to make a good case for positions, even though you disagree with them. This results in a level of comprehension and empathy that will make you a much better advocate for whatever position you bring.*

4. *Keep the discussion on track. Part of your responsibility is to make your remarks relevant. If necessary, explain how your points relate to the discussion at hand. Do your best to make your points while that subject is before the group.*

5. *Speak freely but don't monopolize. If you tend to talk a lot, leave room for quieter people. Be aware that some people may want to speak but are intimidated by those who are more assertive.*

6. *Speak to the group rather than to the leader.*
   Feel free to address your questions or comments to
   a particular participant, especially one who has not
   been heard from or who you think may have special
   insight. Don't hesitate to question other
   participants to learn more about their ideas. The
   discussion should not return to the group leader
   after every point.

7. *Make your needs known to the leader. The leader is*
   responsible for guiding the discussion, summarizing
   the key ideas, and seeking clarification of unclear
   points. But he or she may need input on when
   this is necessary. When you don't understand
   what someone has said, ask. Chances are you are
   not alone.

8. *Speak to your own personal experiences and*
   opinions. Everyone in the group, including you,
   has unique knowledge and experiences. This variety
   makes the discussion interesting and makes learning
   possible for all. But focus your comments on the
   experience you have actually shared. For example, in
   the case of a cancer support group, do not talk about
   the side effects of chemotherapy if you have not
   experienced them. However, you should feel free to
   share your experiences with radiation treatment, if
   you have had it.

9. *Disagree agreeably. Differences will invigorate the*
   group, especially when it is focused on mutually
   shared goals. Don't hesitate to challenge
   the ideas you disagree with. Don't be afraid to
   play devil's advocate provided you focus on the

idea and not the person who presents the idea.
If the discussion becomes heated, the group leader
will intervene. Ask yourself and others whether
reason or emotion is running the show. Keep it
focused on reason, on the ideas.

10. *Remember this is a discussion not a debate.*
    Humor and a pleasant manner can go far in helping
    you make your points. There are not winners
    declared at the end of a cancer support group
    session. In fact, a belligerent attitude will destroy
    the group and any chance you have of learning.
    Be cheerful. Strive to make this a mutually
    supportive learning experience.

Is it...Discussion or Debate?

Cancer support groups thrive on discussion. Debate is something that is saved for the courtroom. We are mutually committed to productive dialog. Understand the differences.

Discussion...
(1) Working to understand each other.

(2) Finding common ground.
(3) Listening in order to find agreement.
(4) Enlarging and possibly changing a participant's point of view.
(5) Evaluates assumptions to reveal truth.

Debate...
(1) Opposing each other and attempting to prove each other wrong.
(2) Winning.
(3) Listening to find flaws and to counter argue.
(4) Defending one's point of view.
(5) Defends assumptions as truth.

(6) Causes introspection of one's position.

(7) Seeks a better solution than any of the original solutions.

(8) Creates an open-minded attitude; an openness to change.

(9) Allows one's thinking to be open to other people's input, knowing the discussion will help improve rather than destroy.

(10) Calls for temporarily suspending one's previously-held beliefs.

(11) Searches for basic common ground.

(12) Searches for strengths.

(13) Involves real concerns for the other person and seeks not to alienate or offend.

(14) Assumes that many people have pieces of the answer and that together they can put them into a workable solution.

(15) Remains open-minded.

Commit to discussion.

(6) Causes critique of the other position.

(7) Defends one's position as the best solution and excludes other solutions.

(8) Creates a close-minded attitude; creates a determination to be right at all costs.

(9) Submits one's thinking and defends it against challenge to show that it is right.

(10) Calls for investing wholeheartedly in defending one's beliefs.

(11) Searches for glaring differences.

(12) Searches for flaws and weaknesses in the other's position.

(13) Involves countering of the other person often focusing on feelings that belittle or depreciates that person.

(14) Assumes that there is a right answer and that they have it.

(15) Implies once-and-for-all conclusion.

About the Authors

Greg Anderson was diagnosed with metastatic lung cancer in 1984. He was given only 30 days to live. Refusing to accept the hopelessness of this prognosis, he went searching for people who had lived even though their doctors had told them they were "terminal." His findings from interviews with over 15,000 cancer survivors form the strategies and action points of this book.

Greg Anderson is author of seven additional books including *Cancer: 50 Essential Things to Do* and the *22 (Non–Negotiable) Laws of Wellness*.

Michael Gingerich is an ordained Elder in the United Methodist Church and has served congregations in central Pennsylvania for 20 years. Among his favorite areas of ministry are teaching, worship leadership, youth work and missions, having led several mission teams to Ukraine and Jamaica. He counts it a distinct privilege to share the hope and triumph that faith in God can bring, experiencing intimately those aspects of faith in caring for a son with autism and mental retardation and with his wife's diagnosis of breast cancer.

For more information and support group services, contact:

Cancer Recovery Foundation
in the United States
www.CancerRecovery.org

in Canada
www.CancerRecovery.ca

Call toll-free (800) 238-6479
in the United States.